Sex. Seems like everybody's doing it.

For sure everybody's talking about it. It's cool! It's great! It makes you feel good, feel loved, feel like you belong to someone.

TV and movies portray it, and rock stars sing about it.

Sex is everywhere today!

But so is HIV . . . and AIDS . . . and twenty-odd STDs (sexually transmitted diseases), some of them fatal—all rampant among young people today.

So here's the question many people today are asking: "Is sex worth dying for?"

Sex, Lies &...the Truth

A MESSAGE FROM
Focus on the Family

Living Books®
Tyndale House Publishers, Inc.
Wheaton, Illinois

Copyright © 1994, 1995 by Focus on the Family
All rights reserved
Cover photograph copyright © 1994 by Jim Whitmer

Living Books is a registered trademark of Tyndale House Publishers,
Inc.

Scripture taken from the *New American Standard Bible,* © 1960,
1962, 1963, 1968, 1971, 1972, 1973, 1975, 1977 by The Lockman
Foundation. Used by permission.

Library of Congress Catalog Card Number 94-61426
ISBN 0-8423-1730-9

Printed in the United States of America

00   99   98   97   96   95
9   8   7   6   5   4   3   2   1

Contents

Acknowledgments

Thanks to Karen Ball, Kurt Bruner, and John Perrodin for their editorial contribution and for the vital role they played in the creation of this book. Also, special thanks to Amy Stephens for her invaluable research and advice.

Special thanks to Robert O. Garner, who wrote, produced, and directed the film *Sex, Lies & . . . the Truth.*

1
Why Not?

SEX. Seems like everybody's doing it. For sure plenty of people are talking about it. They say it's cool, it's great, there's nothing else like it. People say it makes you feel good, feel loved, feel like you belong to someone. You've heard friends talk about it, seen TV and movies portray it, heard comedians joke about it, and heard rock stars sing about it. Sex is everywhere!

With all the emphasis on sex in our culture, it seems strange for anyone to suggest that it might be best to postpone it. And yet, many are saying just that. There is a rising wave of kids who see virginity as a better way to go. Rather than blushing over not "doing it," they take pride in their self-control and self-respect.

It may sound strange to you, but it's true. Teenagers across the country are seeing the consequences associated with sex before marriage and are deciding it is better to wait. They are also realizing that their sexual purity is too precious to be thrown away to just anyone. And no, it isn't because they are dweebs. Some of them are star athletes, school cheerleaders, class presidents, homecoming queens, and just average kids who have more respect for themselves than to get involved in sex before marriage. They've examined the facts and decided it is best to save sex until marriage.

Why would anyone choose to avoid sex when so many voices are saying "go ahead and enjoy it"? In the chapters that follow, we will examine issues that will help you answer that question.

Here are some of the reasons teenagers might give for becoming sexually active:

- To feel good
- To fit in (everybody else is doing it)
- To build self-esteem

- To be popular
- To gain experience
- To get pregnant
- To prove you're a man (or a woman)
- To find out what everyone's talking about
- To avoid rejection
- To feel loved

Do any of these sound familiar? It's not too surprising if they do. Almost everyone has some of these needs. They are a normal part of being human and wanting to be accepted. In fact, sex within the proper relationship is thrilling. But it won't provide the fulfillment some people promise and you might expect if you practice it outside of marriage. Many people, adults and teens alike, who have used sex to fulfill these desires have found that it just didn't do it. They didn't feel accepted or loved, nor did they avoid rejection. Too often, sex gave them the exact opposite experience. They felt cheated.

Unfortunately, they didn't have the whole story. They didn't understand that sex is more than just a physical interac-

tion between two people. Sex involves
your emotions, your health, and even
your intellect—everything you are as a
person.

There is far more to consider when
making a decision about sex than the
allure of media images, pressure from
friends, or even the physical desires of
your body. You must evaluate the facts
and decide what is the smartest path. As
we will see in the coming chapters, there
are very compelling reasons for choosing
to save sex for marriage.

You've heard all the lines before:

- "Sex is the thrill of a lifetime. Why
  miss out?"
- "Everybody's doing it. Why be left
  out?"
- "You don't want to marry someone
  who isn't sexually compatible. Why
  not find out?"
- "Sex with a condom is safe. Why
  worry about it?"

These are just a few of the reasons
you'll hear given in favor of becoming sexually active. But there is another side of

the story. Stay with me through this book, and I'll give you a more complete picture, a picture you won't often see.

JUST THE FACTS
In the pages that follow, we're going to look at the facts, straight and clean. Most of them come from doctors and researchers who are professionals in the field of sexuality and health care. Other facts come from the news or people who watch trends among young people. Much of it comes from scientific studies published in medical journals and by government agencies. There are also comments from real teens about their experiences with sex.

I'll tell you what the professionals are saying and what the statistics are saying. I'll tell you as much as we all know with the hope of helping you make the right choice: Save sex for marriage. When it comes down to it, you are the one who will say yes or no when faced with an opportunity to experience sex. But don't kid yourself. That decision is a very big deal and can have very serious consequences.

The hard truth. My goal is not to scare you. Fear is not a great motivator. But knowledge is, and to make you a truly educated person on this issue, I must show you some unpleasant facts. When I look at the statistics, they really concern me.

INCIDENCE AND PREVALENCE

According to a recent report by the Alan Guttmacher Institute, the research arm of Planned Parenthood dealing with issues of sexually transmitted diseases (STDs) and sexuality in general, the problem of STDs in America is very serious. Specifically, they explain:

- An estimated 12 million new sexually transmitted infections occur every year; two-thirds (8 million) are among women and men under age 25.
- At current rates, at least 1 person in 4 will contract an STD at some point in his or her life.
- As many as 56 million individuals— more than 1 American in 5—may be infected with an incurable viral

STD other than human immunodeficiency virus (HIV), which causes
AIDS.

- At least 31 million people are
  infected with the genital herpes
  virus (herpes simplex virus, or
  HSV).
- 24 to 40 million people are
  infected with human papillomavirus (HPV).
- 1.5 million people are chronic carriers of the hepatitis B virus.
- Between 1987 and 1991, annual
  reported cases of primary and secondary syphilis were at their highest levels in nearly 40 years.
- Gonorrhea is the country's most
  frequently reported communicable
  disease; 620,478 cases were
  reported in 1991.
- AIDS has claimed nearly 195,000
  lives since 1981. An estimated one
  million people are infected with
  HIV.[1]

Let's face it: The news isn't good. Not
by a long shot. And it just keeps getting
worse. The question is why? Why are so

many teens getting infected with STDs? It makes me wonder if young adults realize what's at stake. Are you getting the whole story . . .

about sex?

about pregnancy?

about condoms and STDs and AIDS?

about love?

So maybe you think you have heard it all before. But there's a good chance that you haven't. And if you haven't, then there's always the chance that the thing you don't know could hurt you . . . for a very long time. Maybe even kill you. All I'm asking is that you take a few minutes and look over the material that's available. Yeah, it could bore you to tears.

Or it could save your life.

THE WONDERFUL TRUTH

There are two major reasons why I am so concerned about the subject of sexuality and teenagers. The first reason is what we have already discussed and will discuss in more detail later in this book: Sex can be dangerous. The second reason is that it doesn't have to be dangerous; in fact, it was never intended to be dangerous.

God created sex, and he says it is a very good thing. But we must remember, as the Byrds sing in their popular song "Turn, Turn, Turn," using the Bible as their text, "there is a time for every purpose under heaven." Sex is a wonderful thing if used for its proper purpose at its proper time.

That purpose is for two people to share themselves exclusively with each other, showing love for one another and enjoying each other, and to start a family. The time is in marriage. Sex for any other reason can cause problems. But why, you ask, should it be confined to marriage? Two important reasons, but not *the* most important reasons, are the risks of premarital pregnancies and sexually transmitted diseases. However, let me explain the most important reasons.

Most of you will one day meet a very special person with whom you will want to spend the rest of your life. You will love them more than you ever thought you could love someone. Because you love them and they are so special to you, you will want to give them a very special, one-of-a-kind gift that only they deserve. That gift is yourself and your sexual purity.

Believe me, you will be very glad to be able to give that gift to your husband or wife and say, "All that I am and have is yours, and yours alone." But you can do it *only* if you save yourself. And that is part of what makes it so special. Imagine wanting to give the most wonderful person in your life the most precious gift you can give, but you can't because you gave it away to someone you thought was important . . . but now they are long gone. You can't reverse that tragedy once it has happened; you can only prevent it so that it doesn't. Your sexual purity is much too precious to be given out so easily.

What is more, it is a fact that the best sex is married sex. A recent and very authoritative survey of sexuality in America was conducted jointly by researchers at the Universities of Chicago and New York.[2] These researchers found that of all sexually active people "The people who reported being most physically pleased and emotionally satisfied were the married couples."[3] The researchers also found that not only is sex better in mar-

riage but it is better if you have had only
one sexual partner. They explain, "Physical and emotional satisfaction started to
decline when people had more than one
sexual partner."[4]

A major sex survey conducted by *Redbook* magazine found some interesting
results. Polling approximately 100,000
women, the survey found that women
who were sexually active at age fifteen
are more likely to express dissatisfaction
with their current sex life than those
who refrained from sexual involvement.
It also found that strictly monogamous
women experience orgasm during sex
more than twice as often as women who
have had more sex partners.[5] It may seem
difficult to save yourself for marriage
when marriage seems so far away, but it
isn't that hard (plenty of people do it).
And really, those years are not really that
far away.

This fact of sex being better in marriage leads me to another point, and that
is what people are calling "safe sex." Let
us put aside the fact that there is *no*
really "safe sex" outside of marriage. I
want to talk to you about what sex

should and can really be like. It is important to understand that sex, experienced
in its ideal form, shouldn't have to be
"safe." Sex shouldn't have to be treated as
some science project, making sure everything is just right so nobody gets hurt.
"Safe sex" is a cheap imitation of the real
thing. As one woman said, "Sex can be
many things: dark, mysterious, passionate,
wild, gentle, even reassuring, but it is not
safe. If it is, then it is not likely to be very
sexy." [6] Sex can only be the fabulous experience God intended it to be within the
marriage relationship. It's more satisfying,
guilt-free, and worry-free when it's shared
only with the person with whom you
have chosen to spend the rest of your life.

Take my advice, the experience of millions of men and women, and the advice
of scientists. Save the wonderful experience of sex for marriage; it will be better
if you do, and it is worth it.

THINK ABOUT IT
1. Do you know anyone who has committed themselves to postponing sex until
marriage? How do they feel about that
decision?

2. If you have friends who are married, ask them if they regret or are glad they waited for marriage to have sex? Do they regret *not* waiting?

3. What reasons have you heard people give for becoming sexually active?

4. In light of the statistics given in this chapter, do you think you've been given the whole story about the consequences of sex?

2
The Thrill
of a Lifetime

JILL felt her heart pounding.

She could sense the excitement in the air as she stepped out of the car. Suddenly a dizzying world of lights and sound and activity engulfed her. People were everywhere; laughter rang out from all directions.

"Man, this is gonna be great!" Matt said with a grin, grabbing Jill's arm.

He's jazzed, Jill thought, looking at her friend's face. She could see it in Matt's eyes, feel the barely contained energy in his grip. *Yeah, well . . . why not?*

Jill grinned, too. She couldn't help herself. She'd been waiting a long time for this.

Everybody had been talking about this amusement park—one of the biggest in the country. From the minute she moved into town they had been telling her about it. As she looked around, she couldn't believe it. It was like they all said—it was going to be incredible.

Not that Jill hadn't ever been to an amusement park before. But nothing like this—huge, but with the atmosphere of a carnival midway. She'd never seen so many people, so many lights and rides and booths . . . it was the most amazing thing she'd ever experienced.

EVERYBODY WINS!

"Dollar a dart! Who's gonna be the next winner? Nobody loses; everybody wins!"

The shady-looking carnies were at their booths calling to passersby, tossing out challenges with phony grins.

"Come on, buddy, be a man! Win a prize for the little lady!"

Jill saw a booth right in front of them, and the carnie caught their attention. Colorfully dressed and with a bold smile splashed across his face, the carnie beckoned to Matt.

"Give it a try! Nobody loses; everybody wins."

The whole safe-sex thing nowadays, it's like a carnival game. You know, like the basketball free throw or the baseball toss. They're just a gyp. —Dan

---

She didn't know why, but Jill believed the guy. Maybe it was because the game looked so easy. Knock three bottles down with a baseball. What was so hard about that? Sure, others were walking away empty-handed. But that didn't mean you couldn't win.

You just have to know how to do it right, Jill thought.

"Everybody wins! Give it a try!"

She started to step forward, but Matt grabbed her arm again.

IT'S GONNA BE GREAT!

"Don't waste your time there. Save it for the Eliminator!" And he pulled her along until they were there, standing in front of it. . . . The Eliminator . . . the biggest roller coaster in the United States.

This ride was so big that it had taken several years to build. It was a monster, looming in the darkness like some enormous black metallic creature—waiting for its next victim. Jill's gaze followed the sweeping, glittering twists and turns and watched the cars of screaming people plunge into a corkscrew. Spinning as though out of control, they swept around a curve fifty feet in the air, seemingly seconds before they shot off the edge of the beast.

"Get your tickets here! The thrill of a lifetime! You don't want to miss it!"

With a sadistic grin across his face, Matt nudged her, and Jill reluctantly followed. Her heart was pounding and her eyes shot to Matt. *Can't you hear it?* she wondered, but her friend was oblivious. Jill looked down at the ticket she didn't remember buying—and saw that her hand was shaking.

This is happening too fast! I don't want . . .

"The thrill of a lifetime!"

Matt was climbing into the front seat of the car, that crazy grin plastered on his face. "Come on, Jill! You're not scared or nothin', are you? Don't be a chicken!"

Numb with fear, Jill followed, climbing in next to Matt and reaching for the safety harness almost automatically. Breathing deeply, she settled back into her seat, stared ahead . . . and froze.

She could just make it out in the dark: the first stage of the ride. An incline that seemed to rise forever until it disappeared into the night sky.

What am I doing?!

The thought screamed in Jill's head, but it was too late. The car started forward, the momentum plastering her back against the seat. She gripped the bar in front of her and gave Matt a frantic look. But Matt just waggled his eyebrows as his face glowed with anticipation.

"This is gonna be sooooo great!"

Jill didn't answer. She couldn't. Apparently her voice was the only smart thing in her body because it didn't get in the car with her.

Slowly, steadily, the car moved toward the top of the incline. Then, just as it reached the peak, it shuddered to a halt.

Shaking, fighting the urge to scream, Jill peered over the edge . . . and she knew, suddenly and without a doubt—

"This is crazy! We're gonna die! Get me offa this thing!"

And the car plunged forward.

FOR THE THRILL OF IT

Like Jill and the amusement park roller coaster, you've probably heard about the thrill of sex. You've heard that it feels good and that it arouses passion. You've heard it described as the greatest ride on earth. And when something sounds that good, that exciting, you have to have an awfully good reason for staying away from it.

But roller coasters, scary as they appear, are built to be safe, and amusement park accidents are very rare. Yet no one can say the same about the risks involved in sex; they have never been greater than they are today. The thrills are there, yes, but with sex, the consequences can last a lifetime!

When the carnies of society invite you to play the sex game, it's hard to walk away. The lure of excitement is tough to resist. You want to participate in the thrill of it all. But is the thrill really worth the risk?

There are a lot of things to do in life that are thrilling. But if you're smart, you must consider the risk factor before doing any of them. The higher the risk, the more seriously you should evaluate whether or not the thrill is worth it. Sometimes you will find that the risk is just not worth the chance.

For example, skydiving is exciting. But would you choose to jump from the plane if you were told that one out of five parachutes fails to open when the cord is pulled? Probably not. Or how about rock climbing? Scaling the side of a cliff would be great. But would you climb without a secure rope to catch you if you fell? Unlikely. Waterskiing is a blast. But would you let a speedboat pull you through shark-infested waters? Not if you've got half a brain you wouldn't.

In certain ways, sex outside of marriage is not much different. Sure, it can be thrilling. But you have to evaluate the risks before making the decision to go for it. You may get one of the four perfect parachutes every time you jump, or climb without ever slipping, or ski without ever falling. . . . But then again, you may not. You need to understand why your best bet is to wait for sex until marriage, where it can be the best it can be.

Connie was sixteen when Bob, her boyfriend, convinced her to go to bed with him. Like Matt pulling Jill onto the roller coaster against her better judgment, Connie was pulled into the bedroom despite the fact that she wasn't ready and didn't want to. She hadn't really thought through all of the implications of sex outside of marriage. Caught up in the passion of the moment, she went ahead and took that uncertain plunge. Now she regrets it.

There's more to sex than just, you know, the pleasure and the fun. When you have sex with somebody, you're giving yourself to them. You're giving something to them that you can't get back, no matter how much you want it back. And I think you should just save it for somebody you really care about, and who cares about you, and that you can trust with what you're giving them. 'Cuz you're never gonna be able to get it back.
—Sharri

It isn't that it didn't feel good. It did. But the thrill was over quickly, while the worry lingered for months. You see, Bob had been quite sexually active before

meeting Connie. And there was no telling
whether or not he had one of those sexually transmitted diseases she had heard so
much about. He used a condom, but that
didn't offer her much assurance. Something could have gone wrong—and if so,
Bob could likely be long gone, and
Connie would be the one to pay for it.

It wasn't long before Bob moved on to
another girl, leaving Connie broken-
hearted. You see, like it is for most girls,
sex was more than a physical event for
Connie. It was part of a meaningful relationship, and she thought it would make
the relationship more meaningful. But it
didn't. She gave herself to him, only to be
tossed aside like used goods. The thrill is
over, and now there is nothing left for
Connie but fear, worry, and regret.

Connie was lucky. She didn't get pregnant or infected. Others are not as fortu-
nate. Every day, thousands of young
people play the game of sex—and they
lose. Some find themselves with an unexpected pregnancy, others with a sexually
transmitted disease. All of them face a lifetime of regret for leaping before they
looked. Because the thrill of the moment

seemed so appealing, they lost sight of the risk. In the end, they realized that the game is nothing but a rip-off.

SOMEBODY LOSES

Andrea had grown up hearing that sex outside of marriage was wrong. But she wasn't sure why. You see, convictions that are not based on solid information are not very effective. You must know what you believe and why you believe it; you really cannot take anybody else's word for it. That is why this book will be helpful. It will give you facts so that your convictions about waiting until marriage can have a firm foundation. Well, when the time came, Andrea gave in. She discovered, like many others, that sex isn't always so great.

"It was awful. I didn't feel good afterward. I felt guilty and angry and lonely. Every time he looked at another girl, I knew what he was thinking. At least, I thought I did. I told him we had to stop or at least slow down. We did try to slow down, but it didn't work. And sex didn't make us closer. It pushed us apart. I finally said no more sex, and he said so long. I couldn't believe it. He was so self-ish. I didn't matter at all. Just the sex mattered."

More often than not, the girl suffers most when sex becomes a primary part of the relationship. She takes the biggest physical risk because she can become pregnant and is more likely to get a sexually transmitted disease.[1] But she also takes the biggest emotional risk. You see, girls are wired differently than guys. Guys can move from one physical relationship to another relatively quickly without it bothering them too much. In fact, some prefer it that way. But when a girl gives herself to a guy, it usually means something more to her. Few young women rebound quickly from a broken relationship when sex was part of the package. Someone has said that girls will give sex to get love, while guys will give love to get sex. But it isn't real love—as both Connie and Andrea learned the hard way.

I don't mean to imply that sex isn't risky for guys too. It certainly is. As we will see in later chapters, everyone is at risk for one reason or another. Guys and girls alike can lose the game. Regardless of what they say, everybody doesn't win! More often than not, somebody loses.

> It all happened so fast, Jill barely remembers when the sick feeling started. All she knows for sure is that she was totally embarrassed! She had to rush to the amusement park rest room in order to relieve herself of her lunch. The whole school would be making fun of her come Monday.
>
> Walking out the rest-room door, she gave Matt a sheepish look. Never again will she take his advice. The thrill of a lifetime! Yeah, sure!

THINK ABOUT IT

1. If you were faced with the opportunity to have sex, what issues should you evaluate before making a decision?

2. What could be some of the risks—physical, emotional, and spiritual—of becoming sexually active before marriage?

3. Why is it difficult to consider the long-term consequences of certain actions? Why is it so important?

3
Sex Sells

**A DAY IN THE LIFE OF
TERENCE O'DONNELL**

7:15 A.M.

Caught up in his blanket and a little restless, Terry just barely heard the soft click before the blaring of the alternative rock station KQYT forced his eyes wide open. The beat stamped out any thoughts of sleep as he heard the latest hot song promising "undying love" (to perfect strangers) and lots of sex.

Terry stumbled into the shower humming the lyrics and rubbed his sweaty face with a rough washcloth. He jumped out, toweled off, and smeared on deodorant, hair gel, and some cologne. Ready for the day! Pulling on some old jeans, a T-shirt, and a flannel shirt over it, he yanked the latest rock magazine off the floor near his bed. He had a few minutes before breakfast.

Unconsciously he glanced around, then thumbed to a well-worn section called "Sex Exploits of the Hottest Rockers." He plunged into the familiar stories again, in every detail. He wished there were pictures, too.

For now he'd have to make do with the posters plastered to his walls— young women in thong bikinis showing miles and miles of tanned skin.

8:05 A.M.

"Bye, Mom," he called as he ran out the door to catch a ride with his buddies. Swinging into the gaping doorway of the van, Terry sat back in the seat and listened to the thumping music. Rex slammed the door as they glided away from the curb. Terry grinned and joked with the guys, listening with fascination to a story about the new girl in school—and what she was willing to do on a date. They flew past a billboard for a brand-new adult bookstore and rounded the last corner before they hit the parking lot.

"C'mon, Terry, let's take a look at what they have," Rex said. Terry wasn't sure he should or even wanted to, but—"It's OK. School doesn't start for fifteen more minutes."

Like Terry, all of us are bombarded every day of our lives with sexually oriented magazines, books, films, videos, song lyrics, advertisements, and conversations, you name it. Girls are given the message that they are expected to look and dress like sex goddesses. Guys are given the message that it is their job to enjoy the scenery. Both can be heavily influenced by our sex-crazed culture, but you don't have to be.

The attitude that sex is the ultimate can be seen all over the place. Can you imagine an episode of a show like any of

the popular soap operas, evening situation comedies, or whatever the most popular shows with young adults may be this
week—without some kind of sexual
focus? Not likely. How many times have
you seen a wonderful movie with some
sex scene thrown in that has nothing
whatsoever to do with the story line?
This is because the folks in Hollywood
and New York think that sex sells.

> **Sex is something me and my
> friends are experiencing
> and experimenting with. I
> mean, you see sex every-
> where, in the movies, in the
> ads. If I go out with some-
> body, it's not like I'm, you
> know, interested in that per-
> son. I'm just attracted to
> their body. And that's what I
> want right now. —Juan**

(Do you find it interesting, as I do, that
the same television networks and cable

stations that air these kinds of shows
express grave concern over the terrible
epidemic of AIDS? and that they televise
public-service ads discussing the dangers
of "unprotected sex" and AIDS and HIV—
often during the very shows depicting
the types of behavior they consider dangerous?)

Books, magazines (forget the articles,
just look at the ads! What, exactly, is Cal-
vin Klein selling?), tapes and CDs, radio,
television, movies . . . sex is everywhere.
And why?

It sells! Madonna has built a whole
career on sex—and she's one of the
wealthiest women in the world. Howard
Stern is doing the same.

You can't get away from the messages,
the music, or the images, but you can
reduce your exposure. You can think
about their impact on you. The following
is not a news flash (at least I hope it
isn't): Sexually oriented (or would the correct term be sexually deviant?) material
has not been produced with your good
health and best welfare in mind. It has
been produced to manipulate you. How
can you keep from being reeled in by the

advertisers' schemes? The first thing is to
realize that they do have some control
over you . . . as long as you look at their
ads.

GARBAGE IN . . .

For starters, take pornography. No matter
what form, it promotes unhealthy (and
unhappy) living. Along with being incredi-
bly insulting and degrading to everyone
involved, porn promotes a twisted vision
of sex. Disrespect, rape, and abuse are por-
trayed positively. It's all topsy-turvy—turning what's meant to be good, pleasurable,
and fulfilling (sex) into something cruel,
painful, and empty, and that which is evil
(rape, child sexual abuse, and perversion)
into something that is fun.

Let's just say that it doesn't take a
rocket scientist to figure out that these
images aren't (and can't be!) a part of
healthy lifelong relationships. Ever wonder what happens when we fill up our
minds with garbage that reinforces the
wrong ideas about sex, ourselves, or
others?

Take a look into the prisons and on
sleazy street corners, and you'll have your

answer. A 1988 FBI study found that 81 percent of violent sexual offenders regularly used pornography depicting violence.[1] Garbage in . . . garbage out.

Let's get just a little more specific. Look at some of the popular videos that can be purchased at your local video store. There are movies about teens whose main goal in life is to have sex with as many people as possible. There are others where everyone is sleeping around with everyone else, and the object of the movie is to figure out who is going to match up next. There are movies portraying the most gruesome murders as entertaining. Some kids even base a whole party on these ghoulish exhibits. Depraved minds create fantasies of beautiful, innocent girls being tortured and murdered by evil, sadistic men with names like Jason and Freddy Krueger. They do it for one reason—to make a buck. But it is hardly harmless entertainment. It is well documented that this junk has an impact on those who watch it. Garbage in . . . garbage out.

It's easy to trivialize the impact these films can have on your mind.

"I won't be affected—it won't hurt
me!"

"Everybody knows it's not real!"

"Lighten up! It's just a movie."

Strange thing is, though, just the opposite is true. Here's why: Young teens are in
an important stage of life when it comes
to developing relational skills. You are
forming your view of what makes for a
good, healthy relationship. Forget the sex;
how do you get along with others? How
should you treat them? How do you want
to be treated?

Life imitates art. What we see, we often
do. Because a person on the screen
appears to be successful or sexy by acting in a certain way, we follow right
along; that is why advertisers use sex.
They spend millions and millions of dollars to see what it will take to get people
to buy their product. Many believe sex
will do it. At a subconscious level, we
adopt many of the beliefs and patterns
we observe in others. What we put into
our mind often comes out in our behavior.

The process is so gradual and subtle
that we rarely know it is happening. And

yet, it affects us all. You may think you are becoming a free thinker doing your own thing. But in reality you are merely copying what someone else has put into your mind. In a way, you are a slave to the marketers—we all are to some degree. However, we can limit their power over us by having what Ernest Hemingway said was necessary for every great writer: "a built-in, shock-proof [no-sense] detector" (actually Hemingway used a little saltier language). This means having the ability to tell when someone is trying to snow us or entice us, trying to make us see things their way through trickery and fast-talking. It happens all the time, and the sooner you're aware of it, the better.

Numerous scientific studies show a direct link between what people see in films and how it effects their values. For example, Dr. Dolf Zillman, one the most respected psychological researchers in this field, found that when people were shown mild pornographic movies over and over again, they tended to see rape and other sex crimes as less offensive. Dr. Zillman explains that "even women who had been massively exposed to standard

pornography came to look upon rape as a
trivial offense."[2]

Perhaps the best example and most
obvious illustration of this principle is the
advertising industry. As I said, they spend
millions of dollars to make you associate
their products with a certain feeling,
image, or status. If you wear brand X, you
will be more sexy. If you drink brand Y,
you will be well liked and part of the in
crowd. If you drive brand Z, you will have
all the girlfriends or boyfriends you can
handle. More often than not, they appeal
to your sexual side in an effort to get you
to buy. And it works; that is why they
keep doing it. What we see, we do.

What a setup! We see a film showing a
young man getting aroused by stabbing a
helpless girl. What's the message? Pain
can be a turn-on . . . sex should be violent
. . . wonder what that's like. . . .

I recently heard about a couple of teenagers in New York who decided to imi-
tate a scene they had seen in the movie
The Program. In the film, kids were playing a new version of "chicken"—they
would lie in the middle of the street until
just before an approaching car hit them.

Then they would quickly roll out of the way. The object was to see who could wait the longest before moving out of the car's path. Well, after teens began acting out the scene in real life, Disney decided to pull the movie from theaters.

If the power of suggestion can get otherwise bright kids to do something like that, think of what other areas of your life the media can influence—like your sexual habits and attitudes.

Now, I'm not trying to say that you'll turn into an ax murderer by watching one horror film, or a sex-crazed rapist by watching one late-night cable porn movie. However, it will have an effect on you, and those images will be in your mind forever, played back by your subconscious mind again and again. It is very important to consider how often your attitudes, clothing styles, and actions are influenced by what you see on the television and in videos.

How do you think advertisers find so many people to buy their same old, dull tires, colas, deodorant sticks, chewing gum, coffee, and so on? They tie their ho-hum product to sex and promise you a piece of the action. So you bite . . . and you buy.

But you don't have to take the phony promises at face value. Sure, it's true that the messages about sex are all over the place. But you don't have to read, watch, or listen to them. Be honest: No one is forcing you. Don't let people control your mind. You have the self-discipline to resist. But it isn't easy. Patience, self-control, and a proper focus are not what your natural urges want to foster. Still, it is possible, especially if you are careful about what goes into your mind. Instead of feeding on garbage, try a healthy diet. It will make you a much stronger person.

A HEALTHY DIET

There's an old tale about a man who was trying to straighten out his life after years of messing up. He wanted to do the right thing but found it was a struggle.

He tried for some time to resist temptation and dig himself out of the hole he'd dug for himself. Unfortunately, he wasn't gaining much ground. Finally, frustrated by his inability to do right, he talked with a wise and trusted friend.

"It feels like there's a good dog and a bad dog fighting inside of me," he said. "They're both plenty strong, and sometimes I feel like I'm being torn to shreds as they battle for my will. When the good dog is winning, things are great. But when the bad dog is ahead, everything seems to fall apart. . . . And the bad dog is usually winning. What should I do?"

"Simple," his friend replied. "Stop feeding the bad dog."

Good advice. If we feed our minds with bad stuff, bad actions follow. If we feed them with good, we reinforce what is right. It's simple, but it isn't easy.

It's only natural to want to have sex, to think about and dream about the experience. That desire is something that's been built into the human spirit, and it truly is a wonderful thing when used properly. But you don't have to feed the unhealthy and twisted desires promoted by our "sex sells" culture. You can rise above them and make sure that good, healthy thoughts and images go into your mind. You can win by also concentrating on nourishing the good things in your heart. Feed the part of you that has your best interests in mind. Give your heart and mind a break!

It's not too hard to figure out. Your mind was never intended to be a garbage disposal. If you reinforce what is good by being careful about what you watch, listen to, and talk about, you can beat the odds.

The sex peddlers of our culture bank on your adopting the "herd mentality," doing what everyone else is doing just because it is the in thing. What is encouraging is that there are armies of kids who are showing the world that they are not sex-crazed animals following the herd but rational human beings who have self-respect and dignity.

One of the brightest reasons for hope is a burgeoning youth campaign called "True Love Waits." Teens across the country—by the hundreds of thousands—are making a pledge, a commitment, to sexual purity.

And the movement is spreading beyond everybody's expectations. Support for this "new" concept has come from some unexpected sources. Consider the following: "The point is, you don't lose your mind if you're a virgin. We certainly think that we're capable of managing this behavior. And in this age when everything is so scary, why shouldn't this be a popular option?"

These comments came from none other than talk-show host Phil Donahue during an interview he did with teens (who are committed to practicing abstinence) as part of his program discussing the "True Love Waits" movement.

Donahue made another revealing statement. "Incidentally, a lot of people who came of age in the fifties went to the altar as virgins. Including me." Not only is Phil acknowledging that abstinence is a viable and intelligent option, but he's made a public admission that this was the course he chose for his own life. Donahue says he supports "True Love Waits." Interesting, isn't it? He highlights every kind of perversity on his show; yet, for his own life, he chose to remain a virgin until marriage. Go figure!

"True Love Waits" is the brainchild of a youth minister in Nashville, Tennessee. The idea was sparked when two junior high girls in Richard Ross's youth group shared how they felt as if they were the only two virgins in their entire peer group. Ross, who is also a youth ministry consultant for the Baptist Sunday School Board, wanted to find a way to communicate to abstinent teens that they are not alone—that many of their peers have also chosen to refrain from sexual activity.

He came up with the idea of having teens sign covenant cards pledging to remain sexually pure until marriage, collecting the cards, and then displaying them all at one time to encourage sexually abstinent teens that they are not alone. The Baptist Sunday School Board ran with the idea, which then caught on like wildfire with teens across the nation. In July 1994, for instance, more than 210,000 covenant cards were displayed on the Mall in Washington, D.C. Wow!

If you would like more information about the "True Love Waits" campaign, you can contact the group directly at 127 Ninth Avenue North, Nashville, TN 37234; phone: 1-800-588-9248. Their staff will be happy to help you and provide you with further details about their work.

8:15 A.M.

"C'mon, man, don't be such a goody-goody," they teased. It wasn't hard; they knew just how to get to Terry. They would hassle him until he gave in, so he figured he might as well go along, even though he didn't really want to. But he felt like he didn't really have a choice.

The guys swung open the door of the little newsstand and quickly found themselves looking at rows and rows of provocative magazines. No matter how many times Terry was exposed to those pictures, they always embarrassed and excited him at the same time. He felt his face go red. Something inside told him this was wrong.

What if someone saw him in here? The titles alone would shock his mom, not to mention the pictures inside the covers. But he didn't want to be left out, and he was a bit curious about some of the other magazines. He quickly grabbed one from off the rack and opened it wide. The shop owner kept looking at the ball game on his little television set behind the counter, while not so much as looking up at the kids. He didn't want to scare them away. After all, he knew where tomorrow's customers would come from. He knew that sex sells and it can be addictive.

Terry was late for class again that day, buying for himself another unexcused tardy.

THINK ABOUT IT

1. Do you see the sex messages all around you? What are some examples? How do you react to them?

2. What kind of impact can watching sexually explicit and violent movies have on your mind and actions?

3. Have you ever done something that you didn't feel was right just because others were doing it?

4. What are some of the ways you can feed your mind with positive ideas? How can you give yourself a healthy diet of ideas that won't lead you into sexual obsession?

4
Playing the Field

GRACE had seen herself often enough in the mirror to know she wasn't exactly every guy's first choice for a date, let alone Ken's, who was the hottest soccer player at school. And the best looking. His loud laugh could be heard across the campus, and he had the kind of smile that seemed to be meant just for you.

Not that she'd ever been the recipient of his smiling glance. But she'd watched longingly from a distance. Not only was he gorgeous, he was smart, too.

Grace couldn't believe her bad luck to be standing behind the counter at the Burger Barn, taking orders in a stupid (and hideous) rainbow-striped blouse, when Ken walked in. Hardly a glamorous summer job! She perspired in her polyester even more when she saw Ken choose the line leading to her.

"Hi, Grace." He grinned as he leaned on the red brick counter. She stood there looking . . . and listening.

After she spent several seconds staring without a sound, Ken, looking around nervously, finally probed, "You OK in there?" Feeling like a complete idiot, and sure she looked like one as well, she eventually came to.

"Oh, hi, Ken. What can I get for you?" She didn't mean to sound so eager. She tried to smile as she pushed back a few strands of blonde hair that were always coming out from under her cap.

"Hmmm . . . give me a double-cheese with no onions and some curly fries. I'll have a chocolate shake also." He crossed his muscular arms and looked into her dark eyes. "And say you'll go out for a drive with me Friday night, OK?"

"What? Could you repeat that order?" She struggled for air.

"You heard me, Grace. Please?" His smile infected her, set her at ease. She had to smile back.

"Well, OK." Just as quickly as she agreed, she had a sudden thought. What did she really know about Ken? The answer was written in his incredible smile. *Enough,* she thought, looking into those warm, blue eyes. *He seems so nice.*

Quickly piling up his order on the brown plastic tray—spilling his fries in the process—she pushed it toward him. "See you then. . . . When did you say?" She honestly couldn't remember.

"I didn't, Grace. Let's make it nine. I'll stop by and get you at your house." He waved as he backed away.

"See you later," she said.

PLAYING THE FIELD

You've heard that phrase before, along with so many other tacky descriptions— "taking a test drive" and "checking under the hood" among them. Maybe you've thought it sounded like a good idea—to see exactly how "compatible" you are with someone before signing on the dotted line. Only makes sense, right?

Wrong.

According to *USA Today,* one out of every sixteen teenage girls has a baby each year, and that is up from one in twenty in 1986.[1] In America alone, approximately one million teenage girls get pregnant each year.[2] And increased sexual activity among teens has meant that over 500,000 abortions were performed on teens in 1988, the last available year for these figures.[3]

The way I felt with being alone and dumped and fifteen and pregnant, well, it wasn't important to worry about him leaving me. I had to take care of my child and think about what I'm gonna do for my life and the future of my child's life. —Tammy

---

And pregnancy changes you. When a woman becomes pregnant, something amazing happens to her body, something miraculous. Just ask any woman, young or old, who has been pregnant. Once a woman carries a child, she's never the same again. You can't ignore pregnancy, and believe me, it will have a lifelong impact.

What's more, when an unwanted or unplanned pregnancy occurs, the woman is usually left holding the bag. She almost always has to make the tough decisions on her own because the guy seldom sticks around.[4] Empty promises.

It's just not worth it.

I know it may sound crazy—waiting to have sex until you're married. But actually it's just the opposite. The only true key to having great, totally free sex is to hold out for a relationship that is permanent, committed, and sexually exclusive, and that is found in marriage. Having multiple sexual relationships, whether you do it with one "special person" at a time or with anyone you can get, is cheating yourself (as we saw at the end of the first chapter). Remember, research shows that married people

enjoy sex more than those who are not.
Sure, no one expects to get hurt. But
many do. By pregnancy. By STDs. By AIDS.
By death.

**I have a girl and she's four
months pregnant. And it's
like, I don't know, I think,
*How am I going to support
this kid?* It's going to be
hard for me to support this
baby. —Robert**

LIGHTEN UP!
I can hear the jeers now. "Come on, man.
Lighten up! Don't make such a big deal
over it. It's just having a little fun." Oh,
really?

Playing the field; going for a test drive.
"So what's wrong with that? Sex is great—
yeah, everyone knows that." But the costs
can be high—terribly high.

"The risk is virtually eliminated if you
do it right. The key to safety is a condom.
Right?" Well, not quite. There is a lot of

wrong information going around out
there about the effectiveness of condoms,
and you deserve to hear the whole story.

Assuming you do use the condom correctly—and most people don't—are they
a surefire safety net? Let's look at the facts
for a change. . . .

WHY WON'T CONDOMS STOP
THIS EPIDEMIC?

Condoms are ineffective for a number of
reasons. *First,* laboratory studies show
that condoms themselves are not effective barriers to HIV and other STDs. *Second,* condoms do not provide adequate
protection in actual human application.
Third, (and this is most important) it is
very difficult to get people to use condoms consistently and correctly, as
required by the Centers for Disease Control (CDC), the federal agency responsible
for controlling the spread of diseases,
even with high motivation and aggressive
education. Let me explain these three
very important points.

1. Laboratory studies show condoms are not safe in protecting against HIV.

Dr. Ronald F. Carey, a researcher at the Food and Drug Administration (FDA), tested 89 condoms in a machine simulating sexual intercourse. The condoms were purchased off retail store shelves and represented major brands and styles. He found that at least 29 of the 89 condoms leaked HIV-sized particles in sufficient enough quantities to cause infection.[5] That is nearly a 33 percent failure rate and a poor risk.

The *Journal of Testing and Evaluation* published a study in which 24 condoms were intentionally made defective by piercing them with a very thin metal wire. The holes created by this wire were larger than the size of the HIV virus. Of those defective condoms, 75 percent *passed* the water-leakage test (a common test designed to detect leakage in latex condoms). The study determined that condoms passing the water-leak test "when in use could be capable of passing the HIV virus."[6]

This finding is also substantiated by Dr. Carey in his condom test. Concerning his findings, even though at least 29 of the 89 condoms leaked fluid containing HIV-sized particles, it "is noteworthy that our results revealed no pores large enough to have been rejected by the widely used 300-ml water test."[7]

When teachers or someone on television tells you that condoms are safe because they are tested for holes, you remember what these researchers found and don't be taken in.

2. Condoms are not safe in actual usage. Dr. Susan Weller of the University of Texas, Galveston Medical Branch, conducted a review of data from 11 separate studies on condom effectiveness in actual use. She found that condoms had an average *failure* rate of 31 percent in protecting against HIV. Dr. Weller reports that "since contraceptive research indicates condoms are about 90 percent effective in preventing pregnancy, many people, even physicians, assume condoms prevent HIV transmission with the same degree of effectiveness. However, HIV transmission studies do not show this to be true." Dr. Weller goes on to say that "new data indicate some condoms, even latex ones, may leak HIV."[8]

Dr. Richard Gordon, associate professor, Departments of Botany, Radiology, Electrical Engineering, and Physics (all in all, a pretty smart guy) at the University of Manitoba, reports: "There is already sufficient quantitative evidence to indicate that condoms, as presently manufactured, are inadequate from the point of view of the individual for lifetime protection for the AIDS epidemic, even with training and high motivation."[9]

When used as the sole means of *contraception,* condoms have a standardized failure rate of 15.7 percent over the course of a year.[10] But remember, as Dr. Weller points out, this figure is significantly higher for failure in protecting against HIV and other STDs.

In 1988 the federal government cut off a $2.6 million grant for condom research to the University of California, Los Angeles because "condoms may be incapable of providing protection to study participants."[11] The university was seeking to study the effectiveness of condoms among homosexual men.

In a study of three New York City clinics, 21 percent of female patients with STDs reported that they *had* been using condoms regularly.[12] And it is very important to point out that less than half of sexually active teens use condoms.[13]

What is also very significant is the fact that many STDs can be transmitted from pubic areas that are not even covered by a condom, rendering them absolutely useless as protection. For instance, Kenneth L. Noller, past chairman of the American College of Obstetricians and Gynecology Committee on Gynecological Practice explains, "Several studies have shown that condoms do not protect against the human papillomavirus."[14]

Is it any wonder that at a conference a few years ago of eight hundred sexologists (doctors who study human sexual behavior), not one person raised a hand when asked if they would trust a thin rubber sheath to protect them during intercourse with a known HIV-infected person?[15] Who can blame them? They're not crazy! And yet, some of these same experts are perfectly willing to tell you that you are safe so long as you've got your condom. Yikes!

3. Even adults do not use condoms correctly and consistently, even with education and high motivation. This is a very important point. Even if researchers tomorrow created a condom that did work perfectly, the "golden condom" if you will, that would still not solve the problem. Why? The more important issue is that people don't use condoms. Well, you might ask, "Then don't we need more education to help people use them?" The United States has spent billions of dollars over the past few decades on sex education,[16] and it hasn't worked, as I will show you. Please follow along with me.

Recent studies involving monogamous heterosexual couples, where one partner was HIV positive and the other was negative, are very revealing on this matter. Two particular studies, widely cited by the CDC, revealed that these couples also received aggressive "safe-sex" counseling. With all these favorable factors—high motivation (having sex with a person

known to be HIV positive), aggressive
education (attending "safe-sex" counseling every six months or so), and concern
for the well-being of their partner (these
couples were in long-term monogamous
relationships)—at best, only half could be
motivated to use condoms consistently.[17]
This is not good news for the folks who
think the condom is the answer to these
problems.

Concerning her findings in one of
these studies, Dr. Isabelle de Vincenzi
explains, "The problem is to bring people
to use them [condoms] consistently. I was
quite impressed with the fact that in a lot
of studies of high risk people you often
find that it is quite difficult to have more
than half of them using condoms system-
atically." [18]

Contrast the previous disappointing
results of this highly motivated group
with the feelings of most young people
and adults concerning their risk of
HIV/STD infection. Most people (83 percent), young and old alike, who have sex
with more than one partner believe they
are *not* at risk for HIV and that their
behavior is safe.[19]

This brings up a very serious question: *If the highly motivated group cannot produce significant condom use, how can we expect it from those who believe their behavior is safe?*

The CDC tried to help people use condoms more often by running prime-time condom commercials on television and radio. Perhaps you have heard or seen them, they were on so often. Well, the *Wall Street Journal* reported that the massive campaign "failed thus far to boost condom sales." This was is in light of the fact that, according to the CDC, the condom ads have aired on television some 8,633 times.[20] Maybe it's time for the CDC to try a new approach to the problems of STDs, HIV, and teen pregnancies.

DON'T BE A RAT IN THEIR EXPERIMENT

You probably have enough self-respect to become angry when people lie to you. Well, then, you should demand an explanation as to why you're being told that proper condom use will make sex safer because it supposedly reduces your risks. Safer than what? Less risky than what?

"Reduced risk" actually has very little

to do with you as an individual. Here's why. People who study epidemics look at the big picture and try to figure out how to keep the number of new cases of a particular disease lower than some ideal number. This way the epidemic will hopefully disappear over time. But this doesn't help you at all if you happen to be one of those who become infected. Reducing overall cases is not the same as finding a solution to the problem. Remember the quote from Dr. Richard Gordon, the smart guy. He explains that condoms do not work well for individual protection:

> There is already sufficient quantitative evidence to indicate that condoms, as presently manufactured, are inadequate from the point of view of the individual for lifetime protection for the AIDS epidemic, even with training and high motivation. . . . Therefore condoms provide inadequate risk reduction of the individual.[21]

This means that significant condom use (if it were achievable, and from what we have seen it is not), might reduce the spread over the population, but it offers little assurance to you as an individual.

It is clear that the "safe-sex" message is not working. There is plenty of evidence to show that it is not, beyond the plain fact that more and more people are getting dangerous diseases. Let me show you what some researchers have found out about the effectiveness of the "safe-sex" message.

Consider a recent article in *Family Planning Perspectives,* which is a publication of Planned Parenthood, reporting that sexual involvement among adolescents has increased while condom use has decreased in recent years:

> As adolescent males mature, their sexual activity increases while their condom use decreases. . . . The proportion of respondents who had had intercourse with a female increased from 60 percent in 1988 to 84 percent in 1991. The proportion of young men who used condoms at last intercourse decreased from 56 percent in 1988 to 44 percent in 1991.[22]

Remember that these years, 1988 through 1991, were the years when the "safe-sex gospel" was widely preached by movie stars, comedians, various health professionals, and sports heroes.

What's more, Dr. Douglas Kirby, a prominent researcher in the area of the effectiveness of teen sex education, reports that after examining ten "exemplary knowledge-based sex-education programs," he found that the teens learned a great deal but that their knowledge gains did not help them postpone sexual involvement or use contraceptives when they did have sex.[23]

In fact, *The Atlantic Monthly* recently published a research piece by Dr. Barbara Dafoe Whitehead in its October 1994 issue. The cover of the magazine proclaims, "The Failure of Sex Education." Whitehead claims that there are no hard data to show that comprehensive sex education works and plenty of shattered lives tell us that it doesn't. She answers the "safe-sex, let's-just-get-sex-out-in-the-open" educators this way:

"If free and easy sex talk were a key determinant of sexual behavior, then we might expect trends to look very different. It would be our tongue-tied grandparents who had high rates of illegitimacy and STDs, not today's franker and looser-lipped teenagers."[24]

It doesn't seem to make any sense does it? After twenty years of sex education and billions of dollars, the STD situation has only gotten worse and HIV is on the rise. But, instead of asking, "Are these safe-sex programs the solution or the source of the problem?" the people who decide what you should hear about such things usually choose more of the same: the same old medicine—which still doesn't work.

More of telling you to rely on condoms. More encouraging you to go ahead and play the field. More promoting "protected sex" as the answer instead of the only real solution, the solution most adults seem hesitant to offer, the solution many think won't work because young people won't listen. The only solution that can guarantee your safety. Wait until marriage to have sex.

Ken pulled up to her house and honked his horn. Grace had hoped he

would at least come up to meet her
parents. He seemed about to honk
again, so she ran out to the Jeep and
yanked on the door handle. It was
locked. Ken leaned over and pushed it
open.

"Thanks, Ken," Grace said, smiling.
She looked pretty good, at least for
her, she thought. She waited for him to
say something. Maybe she was too
hard on herself like her mom always
said. Dad always called her "his little
pumpkin" and said she was beautiful.
But what else can a dad say?

"You look hot," Ken said. His eyes
seemed most interested in her bare
back . . . or something more. Grace
squirmed in the seat, pulling the seat
belt across her.

"Don't you wear yours?" she asked,
when she noticed his was still hanging
along the side.

"Oh, sure, thanks for reminding me.
Sometimes I forget—they're such a
hassle." He clicked the belt into place.

Ken reached across the dark space
between them and felt for her hand,
which was on her knee. "We're going

to have quite a night," he promised.

"What have you got planned?" she said lightly. His hand crept its way up her arm, gently touching her waist. Waiting.

"You'll see." That smile shone at her. "Just wait and see."

Ken pushed down hard on the gas pedal, and the Jeep flew toward the edge of town, toward the park at the lake. The view of the moon and stars was incredible. Grace, her parents, and brothers and sisters had gone there for picnics and family birthday parties. What times they had had together.

Unfortunately, it also had come to have a reputation among the local high schoolers and young college couples.

Grace was about to find out why.

THINK ABOUT IT

1. How far should you go on a date? Why?

2. Why isn't sex a good way to test a relationship?

3. What should Grace have asked before

agreeing to go out with Ken? What
should she have known about Ken?

4. If you can't depend on condoms, and
sex education is not working, what is the
best plan of action for you?

5
Is Sex Safe?

PICTURE this. It's been a rushed morning. You woke up late, had to choke down cold cereal and some apple juice, and are now running to school because you missed the bus. The watch on your wrist tells you you're going to make it. Barely. But you've got to keep moving quickly.

So you do.

A block from the school you see a man step out from behind a van. He's holding a humongous box, gift-wrapped with some expensive paper. Those fluorescent, shiny bows—all your favorite

colors—are plastered across the top.
Ribbons pour over the sides. You've
never seen anything like it, except
maybe on TV or in the movies.

It's unbelievable.

And—"It's for you," the man says.
Impulsively you reach out. It fills your
open arms. The man turns and walks
away. You don't know what to say,
what to do. Your parents always told
you never to take candy from strangers. But this is different. This is unbelievable!

Actually, it's wonderful! And it's all
for you.

You place it on the hood of the nearest car, looking around to see if anyone saw you get it—not sure you want
to share. It's kind of heavy. You're
about to rip into the paper and see
what's inside when suddenly you hear
something. Sounds are coming from
deep within the package.

Listen. Can you hear the noise?
What in the world? It sounds like laughter, giggling, and maybe a faint ticking
sound. Nervous, you step back. Then
slowly . . . toward it again.

There they are again. But what to make of it—you have no idea. You've got to find out what's inside. Your curiosity is strong. You pull on the ribbons, and the wrapping paper flops down. Ready to open.

A plain, white box sits there. Do you tear it apart now . . . or later . . . or ever? You mull it over for about half a second and then . . .

A few months ago one of my friends at work got a call from a mother who was very upset about something. She and her young daughter were driving around Colorado Springs running some errands, and her daughter saw a county animal-control truck. The daughter said to her mom, "Hey, look at the sign on that truck. Isn't that dumb?" The sign had a picture of a dog and cat on it, and the caption read something like "Dogs and cats can't wear condoms. Spay or neuter your pet." The young girl was right; it was dumb, but the sign was not the shocking thing. My friend told the mother that the shocking thing was that her young daughter even knows what a condom is when she shouldn't need to know about such things. The mother told my friend, "You know, you're right! Condoms are talked about so often I didn't really think about it. That does make me mad!" Purity and innocence are hard things to hold on to in our sex-saturated culture, where not much is really sacred.

With all the press and attention the "safe sex" campaigns are getting, it's no wonder that even little children know what a condom is. In fact, by the time they reach puberty, most kids will have heard the media and schools push condom use many times over. Too many.

If you're in high school, you're old enough to know whether or not it's OK for you to have sex, right? But really, a lot of high schoolers are making that decision pretty carelessly. And they're getting more than they bargained for. Like a baby or a lifetime infection. A truly intelligent decision is based on a careful consideration of all the consequences involved. When the decision when to have sex is made based on the whole picture, it is clear that the intelligent move is to save sex for marriage.

I can hear your response already: "Hey, that won't happen to me; I'm not stupid," or "No problem; I've got my trusty condom so I'm protected." Maybe. Maybe not. As we saw in the last chapter, the odds are against you.

I think most everybody in high school is having sex before they're married because they don't think of it as a big deal. Not like people before us did. I mean, I don't think condoms are the best message for safe sex, but it's better than nothing. So you might as well try it, I guess. —Brandy

---

For too long now we've heard from many different sources that condoms are the best solution to the problem of teen pregnancy. But the numbers and research don't seem to support that idea, do they? We learned that in the last chapter.

You can see it for yourself. It is naive to

think that condoms will provide sufficient protection against the negative consequences of premarital sex. You may
have read about the "progressive" Colorado school that began handing out condoms. Three years after the school started
its "safe sex" program, "the birthrate [had]
soared to 31 percent above the national
average." In fact, in 1992 they were
expecting one hundred births out of only
twelve hundred students! The administra-
tors at this "cutting edge" school were
described as "searching for explanations." [1] Wow!

**You know, you have the
birth-control pills and the
condoms and all of that, and
that's giving you the excuse
to try and to protect yourself. But it's not true,
because you still get hurt.
—Holly**

It doesn't seem too difficult to figure
out: Giving out condoms encouraged

more students to become sexually active because they believed the devices would make sex safe, and teens feel adults are giving their approval of premarital sex. For instance, a recent report by Dr. Douglas Kirby found that "the greatest number of condoms were obtained, not in those schools where getting them might be anonymous (e.g., through condom machines in bathrooms), but in those locations where there appears to be social support for getting and using condoms (e.g., nurses' offices)." Dr. Kirby explains that this is consistent with other theories.[2] Why wouldn't kids take condoms from machines where nobody would know they were taking them? Because the approval of authority figures (school nurses, teachers, etc.) is so important. That authority can, and should, be used for good—to get kids to save sex for marriage.

When you tell anyone, teenager or adult, that you're going to be handing out free samples of something, very seldom will they refuse. But these free samples weren't just toys or gadgets; they were tools for having sex, supposedly without any physical consequences. We're all told to follow the urges of our hormones: "Just use a condom and have fun."

Think about it. How many of us, teenager or adult, are going to stay away from something that's supposed to make us feel great—whether it's good or wise or not—when we're pretty much assured that there won't be any consequences? Not many.

But there are consequences! That's why we need to hear the truth. Because the sad fact is that these Colorado students—and students all over the place—are not getting the whole story.

As we've already seen, scientific data show that condoms cannot be counted on even to prevent pregnancy. Why? Easy, because they're so difficult to use exactly right. According to the CDC, two of the main reasons for condom failure are incorrect use and lack of use.[3] In fact, another CDC document says just how difficult it really is: "The determinants of proper condom use are complex and incompletely understood."[4]

When you look at a condom, it seems pretty simple to figure out. Take it out of

the package, put it on, and you're all set.
But, it's not that simple. The Centers for
Disease Control (CDC), who are among
those telling us that condoms are a safe
bet for preventing HIV transmission and
AIDS, put out detailed condom use guide-
lines.

Check out this checklist! The CDC tells
us that to be effective, condoms must be
used both "consistently and correctly."

What do they mean by that? Simple: To
use condoms *consistently,* you must

1. "Use a condom with each act of
   intercourse."
2. "Use the condom from start to
   finish."

To use condoms *correctly* you must

1. "Use a new condom for each act
   of intercourse." Though the CDC
   doesn't specifically say so, the condom should be latex.
2. "Put the condom on as soon as the
   erection occurs and before any
   sexual contact."
3. "Hold the tip of the condom and

unroll, leaving empty space at the
end of the condom, yet ensuring
that no air is trapped in the condom's tip." Seems it would be
pretty hard to make sure you'd
done this one correctly in the
midst of a hot-and-heavy situation,
doesn't it?

4. "Adequate lubrication is important,
but use only water-based lubricants. . . . Oil-based lubricants . . .
can weaken the condom." That
means no petroleum jelly or baby
oil.

5. "Withdraw from the partner immediately after ejaculation, holding
the condom firmly to keep it from
slipping off."[5]

In addition, a condom must be fresh, as
well as stored at room temperature, to be
safe and effective—which means a wallet,
purse, or glove compartment is not a
good or safe place to store condoms.

If you think that list is hard to follow,
the Food and Drug Administration (FDA),
the federal agency that tests and regulates

medical devices, recommends an even
more detailed eleven-step guideline.[6]

> **I know most of my friends
> have sex, and abstinence is
> not the answer. I think both
> the guy and the girl should
> protect themselves.**
> **—Elizabeth**

Now, all of this sounds nice and reason-
able when you're reading it on the pages of
a book. But how careful do you think someone is going to be about "consistent and
correct" condom usage when they're in the
middle of a steamy sexual encounter? Not
too careful. The research proves it.

Hardly anyone can meet all the
"requirements" for using these little
devices just the way they're supposed to.
One study shows just how true this is,
and it would be humorous if the consequences weren't so tragic. Dr. Bruce
Voeller, research microbiologist, HIV activ-
ist, and past executive director and con-

tributing founder of the Gay and Lesbian Task Force, found that 23 of 25 males reporting condom breaks in one study used oil-based lubricants. Did these 23 men not use condoms effectively because they were dumb and just didn't know better? Or were they just irresponsible? Not hardly. Of those men participating in Voeller's study, "all had at least a bachelor's degree, two had Ph.D.s; one was an M.D., and another was also a condom researcher." [7] Condoms are difficult for everyone to use properly.

Besides, correct and consistent condom use is only part of the problem. There's also lack of use. Currently, it has been shown that less than half of sexually active teens use condoms.[8] And, as sexually active young men grow older, their use of condoms decreases.[9]

OK. So trusting a condom is risky at best. But what if we did use them right every time (which the CDC admits is difficult, even for highly educated professionals like those in Dr. Voeller's study)? Would they make sex safe? Or safer? Drs. Carey and Weller's separate research shows that the risk for HIV protection is around 31 to 33 percent.[10] Not very good odds.

WANT TO DIE? TRUST A CONDOM

The kick in the head is this: Instead of truly providing protection in relation to STDs, including HIV, condoms may actually contribute to a false and dangerous sense of security. When people think having sex could be dangerous, they are less likely to participate. But, if they believe condoms protect them, they decide it's OK to have sex more often or more easily. "There's little or no danger, so what's the harm? It's not like it's going to kill you."

Problem is, it can do just that.

And then there are the other STDs, such as gonorrhea, syphilis, and chlamydia. More details will follow in chapter 7.

With all the focus on HIV and AIDS, you don't hear as much in the news about these other diseases. Maybe you should. . . . When was the last time you recall reading in the newspaper or hearing on the TV news a story about gonorrhea, HPV, chlamydia, or syphilis? You see, HIV/AIDS is getting all the media attention, but actually you should be more con-

cerned about these other STDs because
they are much more easily spread and
infect more people, and, therefore, you
are more likely to get one or more of
them. And they can cause severe health
problems, pain, problems in conceiving
children in the future, and even death.
For instance, one case of chlamydia can
increase a woman's chance of being infertile by 30 percent![11]

Never let yourself forget this fact: The
physical damage caused by STDs can last
for a lifetime—and can cost you your
future.

Dr. Forrest Smith, assistant director of
the health center at a major university,
treats students for STDs all too frequently.
When he talks with such a student, he
asks the same question: Was it worth it?
So far, out of several hundred students,
not one has said yes.

Dr. Smith explained that most of those
young people figured, "It can't happen to
me." And a lot of them reacted to the
news that they had an STD with "What's
going on? I thought it would be safe if we
used a condom."

Susan was a typical patient. She was

scared and embarrassed. She started out by saying she had a cold, and it took her a while to get to the point. Then she found out how expensive the lab tests were—not to mention the treatment she might need. She asked Dr. Smith not to send the bills to her home.

"I'll pay for it somehow," she told him. Susan didn't want to have to explain to her mother why the tests had to be done.

Dr. Smith's patients suffer even more from emotional scars. "These kids are getting burned," he said. "The result of it all is broken hearts, broken relationships, a sense of vulnerability, frustration, and depression. The girls I see feel ripped off. The guys get mad. But the most common result is the feeling that nobody can be trusted. Condoms are handed out around here left and right. But there isn't a condom for the mind."

Or your heart.

So condoms aren't the answer. At least, not the right one. And neither are any other contraceptives. In fact, Dr. Robert Kistner of Harvard Medical School, the man who developed the oral contraceptive, the birth-control pill, came to the conclusion that the use of contraceptives among teenagers stimulates sexual activity. "About ten years ago I declared that the pill would not lead to promiscuity. Well, I was wrong."[12] What's more, of course, the pill has no effect in protecting against STDs.

Too bad teens are the ones paying the highest price for that error in judgment.

The box is still in your hands. Should you open it or not? There are those sounds again, coming from within the box. The laughter, almost a shriek at times. And what's that—someone softly crying—and that constant ticking, louder and louder with each passing moment. It's all yours. Free! Can you believe someone was willing to just give it to you?

I wonder why? You think about it. There are so many unknowns. The laughter . . . and the sobbing . . . continue.

Maybe it wasn't such a good idea to take this thing. Maybe you should have asked more questions. Yes, definitely. Well, it's not too late. In fact, school is about to start.

You pick up the whole torn mess and haul it to the nearest dumpster. The risk is too high. You toss it over the side. It falls in, the hollow thud echoing.

Turning your back on all the negative possibilities . . . and worries . . . you head for class. And you make it just in time.

THINK ABOUT IT

1. From what you've seen and heard, do you think that promoting condom use increases or reduces sexual activity among young adults?

2. What other reasons are there, besides STDs and pregnancy, to avoid sex outside marriage?

3. Do you think the steps for "consistent and correct" condom use are typically followed? Why or why not?

4. Have you heard much about STDs other than HIV and AIDS?

5. What potential consequences of sexual activity do you think are most serious?

6
The Morning After—Part One

KEN pulled up to a well-worn spot under a canopy of trees, just overlooking the little lake. Grace couldn't help realizing how romantic it all seemed. The night was cool, star-filled—it even smelled right! (And there weren't any mosquitoes!) Everything was perfect . . . but for what, exactly? She wondered.

As the Jeep jolted to a stop, she quickly found out. Ken was suddenly all business; he had a very definite goal in mind. Without so much as a "nice night" or "Do you want to talk awhile?" he forced his mouth over hers. It didn't end there, of course. His hands began to roam all over her. Grace felt excited, the center of attention, but she was scared, too. She liked Ken all right, but she still felt uneasy. It was all happening so fast, way too fast, and she knew that wasn't good.

She shoved him back and could see his smile had been replaced by a completely different expression. "What's wrong?" he blurted out. "I thought you liked me."

"I do," she said quickly. "At least I think so."

"What's that supposed to mean?" he barked. Then, realizing his error, he smoothed out his lined forehead and said, "Come on, it'll be fun."

"Wait a minute," Grace said. "I'm not sure."

"Well, make up your mind quick," said Ken, jamming the key into the ignition and cranking the starter.

"OK, OK," she said. "Calm down, Ken."

"Yeah, right . . . there's nothing

wrong with me." He smiled. "I was just getting a little worried about you." He pulled her toward him, locking her into his arms.

Grace closed her eyes and waited for him. Ken eagerly complied.

Tough decisions . . . and they are decisions that you will have to make or are making now.

Beautiful twenty-two-year-old college student Jenny thought that condoms were the answer. She made sure her boyfriends were always considerate enough to use one. And they did.

One day Jenny noticed a small growth on her genital organs. A biopsy showed this to be a sexually transmitted precancerous lesion. In other words, if Jenny hadn't noticed this growth or done anything about it, she would have required surgery or even worse.

Jenny couldn't understand how such a thing could have happened to her because she had her partners use condoms every time. Her problem most likely was due to the fact that beyond condoms not being effective as devices, condoms cannot protect against some STDs. This is because they are spread from pubic areas the condom doesn't even cover, rendering even a perfect condom useless against these STDs.

Kenneth L. Noller, past chairman of the American College of Obstetricians and Gynecology Committee on Gynecological Practice explains, "Several studies have shown that condoms do not protect against [HPV]."[1] Another doctor has explained that "because HPV is a disease of the entire genital area, condoms probably do not prevent transmission."[2] Jenny just couldn't understand how such a bad thing could happen to her when she had been careful enough—good enough—to practice "safe sex." But obviously "safe sex" wasn't safe enough.

Beyond the serious problem of STDs, there is another consideration: the risk of premarital pregnancy. If you get pregnant while you're in high school, you will be faced with some tough choices. You've basically got three options: Have the baby and raise it, have the baby and give it up for adoption, or end the pregnancy through abortion.

Here's a chance to take a closer look at these three choices.

Choice #1: I'm going to keep and raise my baby. If you take this option, be prepared to put your own dreams and desires on hold for a long, long time. Plans for college? You can probably forget them . . . along with parties, free time, and sleep.

Have a career in mind? Pretty tough to make it happen without a good education. Like most teens who choose to keep their babies, you may well end up feeling trapped, as though your life was cut off before you really had a chance to experience it. You will go from being young and free to being tied down, responsible, and "on call" for the next eighteen years or so. When you have a baby, your life is no longer your own, and that is fine for adults, but not for a teenager. You have to think of the baby first, take care of the baby's needs, lose sleep for the baby, find ways to make money to support the baby . . . and on and on and on. It will require you to be an adult when you should be enjoying being a teen.

Of course, you may not have to face this option alone. Your parents can help and support you, as can the father of your baby; however, more unwed fathers are

---

I was best friends with this guy, and one day he knew that I liked him so we went upstairs. He asked me if I wanted him to stop, and I said no. Maybe a year or so later, we had my son. My boyfriend—my ex-boyfriend now—does not share in taking care of my child. He wants to but he's not really doing anything for himself so I don't see how he can do anything for our child. I mean, there's a lot I wanted to do . . . go away for college and stuff. But, if I do that, I can't take my baby with me. It—it's just holding me back from a lot of things I wanted to do. —Mika

---

not likely to.[3] If the father is interested in you and his child, you could get married. Not all marriages that start on the basis of an unexpected pregnancy fail. Many do, but not all. Some young couples decide they love and respect each other enough to face the future together. To do this, they must forgive themselves for the mistakes they've made, learn and profit from those mistakes, and get on with their lives together. It is far from easy to make a marriage work with this kind of start . . . but it has been done.

In addition, there are organizations and ministries throughout the nation that provide nurturing and practical care for unwed mothers, including counseling, lodging, financial aid, and opportunities to grow spiritually. Some of these ministries can even help you arrange for an adoption, which is the next option that you'll have to consider.

Choice #2: I'm going to give my baby up for adoption. Adoption can be a very positive option for a teenage mother; in fact, for most it is the best option. It is a win-win situation for both the birth mother and the adoptive parents who desire to have children to raise. There is also an overwhelming amount of scientific research to show that children do much better in all areas of development when they are raised by two parents.[4] Adoption provides that advantage for the baby of a single mother.

When I got pregnant, I had dated this guy for a year and a half. I thought, of course he'll marry me. We're in love. We've dated a year and a half. He took off. —Beth

---

However, even though adoption is a very positive alternative to a problem pregnancy, you should understand that it is not an easy option. You are going to take nine months out of your young life to carry this child. After you have carried the baby for this time, there will be childbirth, which is difficult enough for an adult, much less a single teenager. And even though it is usually the best thing, it is difficult to give up that child you have become attached to while it was growing in your womb.

It would be much easier for you to make sure that you never have to make such a hard decision. The only way to do that is to wait until you are married to have sex. That way you can be sure that your baby will have a daddy that is around and is able to be involved in your son's or daughter's life. I'm not preaching to you; I'm just telling you what is smart and makes sense. I have included a section at the back of this book that will tell you about good adoption agencies if you should ever need this information for a friend. See appendix A.

Choice #3: I'm not going to have this baby. Then there's the third option: to end the pregnancy by abortion. Many people may tell you that this is the simplest, most convenient solution to an unwanted pregnancy, and many people believe this. Some women seem to consider it another form of birth control. Over 500,000 abortions were performed on teens in 1988, the last available year for these figures.[5]

On the surface, an abortion would seem to take care of the situation by "terminating" the unborn baby and cutting off all future responsibility to nurture and care for the child. But what many women don't realize is that having an abortion can create even more difficulties than proceeding with the pregnancy. Many women who have had abortions will tell you that it is much easier to remove a baby from your womb than it is to remove that baby from your memory. Once the procedure is over, the thoughts of what that child might have become linger on for years, and those thoughts can cause serious psychological problems. According to Dr. Vincent Rue of the Institute for Pregnancy Loss, one of the most respected researchers on the issue of the negative psychological effects of abortion, women who have abortions face a number of negative consequences after their abortion. According to Dr. Rue, here are what some researchers have found:

- The *Journal of Social Issues* examined the psychological effects of abortion and concluded, "There is virtually no disagreement among researchers that some women experience negative psychological reactions post-abortion."[6]

- Another study showed that "women who obtained abortions are at higher risk for admission to psychiatric hospitals than are women who delivered."[7]
- One study revealed that women who had aborted later felt suicidal (33 percent), had flashbacks (61 percent), experienced negative reactions on the anniversary of when their delivery date would have occurred (54 percent), and showed sexual difficulties (59 percent).[8]
- In another study, 100 percent of the women reported feeling depressed, 92 percent felt anger, 92 percent felt guilt, and 81 percent had preoccupations with the aborted child following their abortions.[9]
- What young people must realize is that the abortion procedure affects

adolescents more severely than it affects adults. Adolescents are more likely to be suicidal, have poorer relationships with others and feel guilt, depression, and isolation after their abortion than are adults.[10]

• What is more, doctors are now reporting that abortion could increase a woman's risk of breast cancer in later years.[11]

Combine all of that with the fact that by the time you know you're pregnant, your baby is already developing. This is not a blob of tissue we're talking about here. From the moment of conception, a wonderful chain of events takes place. A new human being has been created, and nothing new will be added to this creation—except time and nutrition. These are the only two things that have changed your physical makeup since the moment you were conceived by your parents.

According to Dr. Joe McIlhaney, Jr., an OB-GYN specialist, the baby in the womb is a human being who has a heartbeat around 21 days after fertilization. At 28 days the baby is 10,000 times larger than it was at fertilization. It is really growing fast, isn't it? Its arms and legs have already started to develop. At 35 days the eyes are forming, and soon the ears, nose, lips, and tongue can be recognized. At 40 days the brainwaves can be detected, recorded, and read by a doctor.[12]

We must realize that life, all human life, is precious because it is given by God and must be afforded highest value. We must also realize that abortion doesn't ever just fix a mistake; it takes a life and creates more problems.

WHAT ABOUT THE GUYS?

You've probably heard it plenty of times: Men and women think about sex in very different ways. Women are generally motivated by the relational side of sex, by loving and being loved. For women, sex is as much an emotional experience as a physical one. Many men, on the other hand, look at sex more as a physical experience. For the most part, outside of marriage, guys are more interested in the act of sex, whereas girls are interested more in the relationship.

As we have pointed out in chapter 1, when two people are married, sex is different. It is usually practiced for a different reason: because the man and the woman love one another and want to show that love to the other person. What's more, sex is better for married couples, and the research shows it, as we saw in chapter 1. For unmarried teens, however, sex is more likely to be a selfish act where each is trying to meet their own individual needs. This has something to do with why sex is better in marriage.

Because of these differences in unmarried and married couples, they are going to respond differently to the consequences of sexual activity. When faced with the news that a "good time" ended up producing a baby, most young men will back out of the relationship. David Blankenhorn, one America's most noted authorities on the role of fathers, explains that for the first time in our nation's history, millions of men are choosing to escape their responsibility as fathers. He explains that the principle cause of fatherlessness used to be death; however today, "the principal cause of fatherlessness is paternal choice."[13] And that means that millions of mothers are left to raise their children by themselves.

Sometimes young men, in an effort to "do what's right," *will* marry the girl and quit school. But, as mentioned above, this often makes the problem worse because, without an education, it is unlikely there will be many opportunities for good-paying jobs. As a consequence, the young couple is caught in the trap of a low income and usually a growing family, without any hope of improving their situation. Desperation, anger, and hopelessness all become familiar companions.

A lot of men who are becoming fathers today share another challenge: a lack of healthy role models. When a boy's father is absent or can't come to terms with all the implications and responsibilities of fatherhood (and both are happening at alarming rates according to Blankenhorn), the boy grows up without any practical, day-to-day idea of how to parent his own children in healthy ways. For such young men, the idea of suddenly becoming a father is terrifying, to say the least. Not only are they responsible for the financial support of a family (usually before they are equipped to fulfill that responsibility), they are suddenly the source of emotional support for a wife and child.

I went to tell her I was sorry. For getting her pregnant. For freaking out when she told me. But she was gone. Her whole family. Just gone. Moved away. And she never called me or told me what she did. I started to think about it, you know, about having a kid. A son. Or a daughter. Man, I really wanted to see that baby. Maybe she got rid of it. But I'll never know. And that can drive you crazy, thinking that maybe you've got a kid out there somewhere and they don't even know you exist. —Bobby

---

What is more, young men (and women) who are trying to derive from sex emotional satisfaction and security, a feeling of being wanted and loved, are not ready to play the role of parents.

But sometimes, the father will want to be involved and he is not able to because the mother prefers it that way, or her parents exclude him from the decision-making process. This is why it is important to make sure that you are married to the mother of your child-to-be before you seek to conceive one. That way, nobody can limit your rights as a father. That is the way God planned it.

One more thought about whether or not the guys are taking less of a chance than the girls. As we will see in the next chapter, both are at high risk for sexually transmitted diseases. So whether the girl becomes pregnant or not, guys have some serious issues to evaluate when it comes to sexual activity.

THINK ABOUT IT

1. Whom do you think typically pays most when sex leads to an unexpected pregnancy, the girl or the guy? Why?

2. Which of the three choices seems the

best response to an unplanned pregnancy? Why?

3. How can you avoid having to choose any of them?

7
The Morning After—Part Two

LET'S take a closer look at another possible "morning after" discovery—sexually transmitted diseases, or STDs as they are sometimes called.

The truth is that your body can become infected with a number of ugly and painful diseases that are transmitted solely through sexual contact. Not a pretty picture, but you really should know about the dangers. Here are the facts on STDs. You've probably heard plenty about them in school, but you haven't heard it all.

Not too long ago there were just five

STDs that anyone had to really worry about.[1] Now, according to the CDC, there are over 50 organisms and syndromes that are recognized as being sexually transmitted.[2] The CDC reports that 12 million new infections from STDs occur each year.[3] Three million of these cases are teenagers, and 63 percent of all reported STD cases affect people less than 25 years of age.[4]

Consider the following statistics:

- Human papillomavirus (HPV) is associated with over 90 percent of the cases of cervical cancer, which in turn kills 7,000 women a year—more than die of AIDS.[5] In 1991, HPV rates were as high as 38 to 46 percent among adolescent and young adult females in certain settings.[6]
- In 1991, the World Health Organization estimated that up to 5,000 people become infected with the human immunodeficiency virus (HIV) every single day worldwide. Since 1989, the number of 13-

to 24-year-olds with AIDS has increased by 77 percent.[7]

- Chlamydia infects as many as from 2 to 40 percent of women in the United States, depending on the population screened. It is a major cause of tubal infertility. The virus is oftentimes present without physical symptoms, making it hard to diagnose and treat.[8]
- Infection rates for syphilis in the United States are 134,000 a year and are at their highest levels in 40 years.[9]
- Hepatitis B infection is increasing throughout North America and is occurring frequently in adolescents.[10]

Those diseases and viruses with the funny sounding names you heard about in sex education class are still here. And they are growing. Like a muscle you use over and over until it's rock hard, they're getting tougher and becoming more dangerous than they were before. And some of them are becoming resistant to the antibodies that were once used to cure them.

We thought some of them were no longer a problem, like syphilis, for example, but now they have greatly increased in frequency.

They are coming back with a vengeance. There are now many new cases of syphilis, which up until a few years ago was almost considered an infection of times past. And there are some strains of gonorrhea that are resistant to penicillin, leaving the infection free to destroy reproductive organs if an alternate antibiotic is not used.

It's not bad enough that these diseases can make your life miserable. Some STDs are caused by viruses, which means once you get it, it comes to live in your body . . . and it's never leaving. Any pleasure that one sexual encounter gives you lasts only for a moment. The consequences could last a lifetime.

So, what are the current STDs? Here's a list of the names and effects of the most common:

Infectious Diseases
- Syphilis—This disease rivals only AIDS as the most dangerous sexu-

ally transmitted disease and is only
acquired by having sex with someone who has the disease. Without
a blood test, it is very difficult to
detect in women. The first sign is
usually a painless sore at the place
where the infectious organism
entered the body. It usually develops
from ten to ninety days after the sexual contact took place. It may take
the form of a pimple, a blister, or an
open sore. This sore usually goes
away within two weeks, but it has
only gone "underground" to do its
more insidious and long-term work.
It will develop and can cause hair
loss, rashes, hepatitis, kidney disease,
meningitis, changes in the bones of
the body, and eye infections.[11] What
is more, congenital syphilis (contracted by babies in the womb of an
infected mother) kills 40 percent of
babies born to infected mothers. If it
doesn't kill the baby, it can cause serious deformities or even blindness.[12]
- Gonorrhea—This pus-producing
  bacterium is passed primarily by
  sexual contact. It is more common

than syphilis. In fact, gonorrhea is the country's most frequently reported communicable disease; 620,478 cases were reported in 1991.[13] As many as 100,000 women are made sterile by gonorrhea each year in the United States.[14] It is much more dangerous in women than men. In men, it can cause scarring and abnormalities of the urethra. In women, it can cause scarring, pelvic inflammatory disease (PID), and sterility. A one-time sexual contact with an infected person brings a 40 percent chance of contracting the disease.[15]

- Chlamydia—This is spread only by sexual intercourse. It primarily infects a woman's uterus, tubes, and ovaries. Women who are infected with this organism may not know it for some time. In fact, Dr. Joe McIlhaney, OB-GYN and president of the Medical Institute for Sexual Health, explains that 70 percent of women who have this infection are not even aware of it. Chlamydia is also a major cause of ectopic pregnancies (where the baby grows in the fallopian tubes, rather than the uterus). This is because chlamydia causes pelvic inflammatory disease (PID). The rapid increase in chlamydia infections is believed to be the primary reason why ectopic pregnancies have increased five times since 1970.[16] This is important if you plan on having a family one day.

Viruses

- Herpes Simplex II—Most common cold sores are caused by a form of herpes. That is herpes simplex I, and there is an important difference. Herpes simplex II is a sexually transmitted disease caused by a virus that produces blisters and sores in and on the sexual organs. The virus does not remain at the site of original infection. Type I can be transferred to the genitalia by oral intercourse, and, likewise, type II can be transferred to the mouth the same way. In both men and women, the outbreaks of either

can also occur anywhere on the
skin if it is irritated or broken. It
will, once beneath the skin, invade
the body and finally lodge in a
group of nerve cells called the dorsal nerve root ganglia. (You might
want to remember that if you are
ever on *Jeopardy* . . . "Alex, what is
the dorsal nerve root ganglia?")
Herpes blisters are extremely painful and can hinder simple bodily
functions like urination.[17]

If an infected woman has herpes sores
present at the time of a vaginal birth
(either type I or II), the virus can get into
and infect the baby's body. Even though
this transmission is rare, studies show that
70 to 100 percent of babies who actually
contract herpes this way will die or have
severe neurological damage due to the
infection.[18]

• Hepatitis B—This very common
  STD is caused by a virus that is
  transmitted through bodily fluids
  (blood and blood-derived products,
  semen and vaginal fluids, and

saliva). One and half million people in the U.S. are chronic carriers of hepatitis B. This virus affects the functioning of the liver and can often cause damage severe enough to be fatal. You can be a chronic carrier for many years without knowing it, and so can your mate.[19]

- Human Papillomavirus—HPV causes soft venereal warts, which are associated with genital cancer in both sexes. Roughly seven thousand women in the U.S. die every year from genital cancers related to HPV.[20]

One young woman, a twenty-five-year-old college graduate, tells her own story:

While I fully acknowledge my grave error and sin and suffer for it daily, I feel someone must warn the teenagers, the single young adults, and anyone else contemplating a sexual encounter that they will later regret it. The government and media have thoroughly communicated about AIDS; that is not what this letter is about.

I'm writing about my concern over what Human Papillomavirus (HPV) can do. It can give cervical dysplasia, leading to cancer of the cervix in teenagers. Certainly this is tragic. But it has many other effects that I have not read anything about. I have had the best physicians available, and they have given up on me. There is no cure and no way out.

At twenty-five, I have remained single and childless. That singleness is imposed upon me by my physical condition. The last four years of my life have been lived with chronic pain, two outpatient surgeries, multiple office biopsies, thousands of dollars in prescriptions, and no hope. The effect of this problem is one of severe, relentless infection. This condition can be so severe that the pain is almost unbearable, and a sexual relationship (or the possibility of marriage) is out of the question. The isolation is like a knife that cuts my heart out daily. Depression, rage, hopelessness, and a drastically affected social and religious life are the result. While I may not be one of the success stories, I am managing to survive, and it is my hope and prayer that someone will make HPV as well known as AIDS. It took me months to get a diagnosis. . . .

Attempts at a cure are not undertaken in a comprehensive way by the medical profession. My confidence is pretty well shattered. Physicians say they are seeing HPV more commonly. Females are being sentenced to a life of watching others live, marry, and have babies—none of which they can do themselves.

Please take what I've said to [others]. Thank you for listening.

The virus HPV, which is associated with cervical cancer in this young woman, is killing thousands of women each year—far more deadly than AIDS.[21] And yet it wouldn't be too surprising if you've never heard of HPV. HIV and AIDS are getting all the publicity because they are terrible problems. But even more terrible are all the other STDs we just discussed that are a greater threat to sexually active people outside of marriage. They are more of a threat for two reasons. One, because people are not being told about them, and therefore many people are not aware of their danger. Two, these diseases are much more easily transmitted than HIV is. Therefore, your chances of getting one of these other STDs is much greater than getting HIV. For instance, consider HPV. Twenty years ago doctors seldom saw precancerous conditions in people in their teens or their twenties. Today, it is an everyday occurrence, the fastest growing sexually transmitted disease in the United States.[22] But remember, your chances of catching any of these are significant.

And yet HPV and the others could be eliminated, wiped out, if uninfected people would wait until marriage for sex, find and marry an uninfected partner, and remain mutually faithful for life. That's all it would take. And the solution could start with you.

- Human Immunodeficiency Virus
  (HIV)—This is carried by more
  than one million Americans, taking

over 250,000 lives since 1981.[23] It has even surpassed accidents as the number one killer of young adults.[24] To date, there's nothing to cure HIV once you have it and no vaccine on the horizon to protect you from getting it. And don't think you have to be a homosexual or drug user to contract HIV. The most rapid increase in HIV cases in the United States is among heterosexuals.[25]

Death from AIDS is extremely painful with unimaginably complex infections and cancer, often accompanied by severe weight loss, diarrhea, and loss of intellect. It is a very ugly sight. This is why the death experience of AIDS victims requires extreme and loving compassion from the Christian community. There are local hospices that need people to do everyday tasks for AIDS patients like reading to them, running errands, or just talking. Look one up in your community, check it out, and offer a hand.

- Acquired Immune Deficiency Syndrome (AIDS)—This is a viral infection caused by HIV. It breaks down your immune system so that you cannot fight off diseases. It leaves you vulnerable to the thousands of diseases that a healthy body is able to fight off.

First, a few questions. How likely is it that you could get AIDS? Who's at risk? Is AIDS really that bad? After all, when NBA superstar Magic Johnson first announced

> **The students I'm working with don't look at AIDS as something that would happen to them. And even if the young people do contract AIDS while they're in high school, most probably won't show signs of the disease until they're well out of college.**
> **—Marci Farrington-Delgado, health education specialist, L.A. Unified School Districts**

he had the virus that causes AIDS, people freaked out.

The volume of calls to health clinic hotlines went crazy. People figured if someone like Magic could get the disease, anyone could. Then just a few months later, Magic was named MVP at the NBA All-Star Game. Not only was he still playing, he was the best of the best!

Now folks were really confused. If AIDS was so horrible, how could an infected person look so good and play so well? What was the truth about this disease?

Dr. John Dietrich is a board-certified infectious-disease specialist working primarily with diseases that are contagious, like AIDS. In fact, he treated hundreds of patients with AIDS during the first ten years of the epidemic. Based on his experience, here are a few things that he considers to be true about AIDS:

- You don't want to get this disease. AIDS is a terrible, slow, and sometimes excruciatingly painful way to die.
- You don't have to get it if you don't have it already. Getting AIDS

> isn't a matter of race, age, gender, or even sexual orientation. It's mainly a matter of behavior: what you do and don't do.

- HIV, the virus that causes AIDS, is spread in only three ways: through sex, through exposure to blood and blood products, and from a mother to her baby.

As Dr. Dietrich explains in his book *The AIDS Epidemic: Balancing Compassion & Justice,* viruses are very small organisms that can cause diseases like colds and flu.[26] You've probably had plenty of viral infections in your life—flu, chicken pox, measles. They haven't been fun, but they

---

"It scares me, about getting AIDS."
  "Yeah, you can have sex, and then you can die."
  —Tyler and Max

---

haven't been life-threatening either. So what makes HIV and AIDS different?

Your body's immune system is constantly alert for potentially harmful invaders (microorganisms) that try to make you sick. HIV attacks your immune system, the system that protects you from diseases, and weakens it, making you vulnerable to certain diseases that healthy people don't normally get.

One type of white blood cell is called a lymphocyte. Lymphocytes have helper and suppressor cells called T-helper cells that work with other cells to recognize surface molecules (antigens) of invaders and immediately launch a counterattack. But HIV tricks these guardians of health by implanting its genetic material inside them, controlling their activity and effectiveness.

The most treacherous thing about HIV, though, is that it doesn't act like most viruses and cause disease quickly. You know how fast colds and the flu hit you. Seems like you just start to feel achy and feverish, then you're down for the count. HIV, after some initial reaction, may then cause no further symptoms for years. During this time, an infected person may seem totally healthy—may not even know they are sick. For instance, one study done in San Francisco by Dr. George Lemp found that 70 percent of the participants in his study were *unaware* of their positive HIV-infection status at entrance into the study.[27] The trouble is they are infecting people without knowing it.

So with HIV, millions of people can be infecting millions of others, who will infect millions of others, without anybody knowing for years that they have acquired a fatal disease.

So what does this have to do with you? Nothing, if you don't have sex until you're married; if you and your spouse are both virgins or uninfected when you marry; if you stay faithful to each other throughout your marriage; and if you don't inject drugs and avoid other activities that bring an infected person's blood, semen, or vaginal fluids into your body. (Are you seeing

---

Life is short, but if you get AIDS, it's even shorter.
—Vinay

---

some patterns here when it comes to truly safe sex?)

But if you are considering having pre-marital sex, then it may very well have everything to do with you.

TRANSMISSION OF AIDS—SOME MORE DETAILS

As Dr. Dietrich explained, HIV is spread through sexual transmission, blood transmission, and birth transmission. So far, about 70 percent of HIV cases in the U.S. have been transmitted through sexual contact.[28] Homosexual practices more easily spread HIV because of multiple partners, anal intercourse causing increased trauma to the lining of the anus, and the fact that homosexuals often have other STDs causing skin sores, which make it easier for the HIV to enter the bloodstream. But remember, HIV is increasing steadily among heterosexuals.

You *don't* get AIDS through casual contact. You can't get it from a toilet seat or restaurant silverware, being in the same classroom, hugging or touching, being coughed on, shaking hands, or even from kissing (though deep kissing may not be safe).[29]

But take a look at those percentages of transmission again: About 70 percent of AIDS cases in the U.S. have been acquired through sex. Seventy percent! The sexual revolution lives on, whispering that sex is OK between consenting partners as long as nobody is hurt. But a lot of people *are* getting hurt. And a lot of people are dying.

All of these diseases, and a whole host of others, can be transmitted during sex by people who don't even know they're infected! They don't look sick. They don't feel sick. But they can be dangerous.

What's even more unnerving is that your very first experience with sex can kill you if your partner has HIV. I don't say that to scare you, but to be realistic. And there's really no sure way for you to know if that person is infected. If they have been sexually active, it is entirely possible that the person is infected without knowing it. Is it worth it?

> "Did you have a nice time, Sweetie?" her dad asked as he sat on the edge of her bed, like every night before. At

times she felt foolish when he gave her a big hug, but tonight she wanted to be a little girl again. Grace couldn't say a thing in answer. Her throat felt tight, her face was burning up. Could Dad see how red it was?

"Sure, yeah! Ken's pretty fun to be with!" she finally managed.

"Good night, honey." Her dad paused and looked at her, smoothing back those strands from her forehead. "Anything you want to talk about?"

Grace snuggled into her pillow. "No, thanks," she said. "I'm really tired."

Nothing would ever be the same for Grace. Sure, she knew tomorrow would come, but she wondered what it would be like for her. What in the world was in store? Would she experience any of the possible morning-after regrets . . . or consequences?

She'd have to wait to find out.

THINK ABOUT IT

1. How do you think you would react to the discovery that you've contracted an STD during sex with your boyfriend or

girlfriend? Or that you might have given one to someone else?

2. In light of all the possible morning-after consequences of sex, is it really worth the risk?

3. Why are the diseases, other than HIV, more of a danger to you?

4. Why is HIV spreading so quickly through our population?

8
Too Late?

THE ambulance tore around the corner, red lights flashing, siren screaming. The street dipped, and the medic team bounced, their heads just missing the ceiling. They were used to flying along rough roads at breakneck speeds and were ready for anything as they neared the accident scene. Up ahead they saw the fire truck and the badly battered car.

"Company 12 has started already," the driver said to the others.

"That's good," Tracy said. "Maybe we'll have it easy tonight!" The group laughed to relieve some of the pressure as the van pulled up to the scene of the accident.

Steve had a high plastic collar around his neck, and Tracy yanked out a stretcher to carry him with for the ride to the hospital. Two of the team quickly lifted him onto his "bed" and pulled tight the belt that crossed Steve's chest. They cranked down the other belts at his waist and over his legs. Steve felt like a refrigerator on a mover's dolly.

Blood dripped down in sticky streaks along his throbbing forehead as he tried to give—for the third time—more details about "where it hurt." He looked at the round lights hovering above him. To the police officer he again recited the story—that red car swerving, the sound of glass shattering.

The thick board they had him stretched out on made his neck ache more than ever. Steve squirmed to get more comfortable. It just wasn't possible.

Eyes barely focused, he called out

for his father. The sound was hardly a squeak. "Dad," he said weakly, his voice hoarse and throat aching.

"Rest now, kid," the man said.

"Your father has been called," another paramedic assured him. Steve's thoughts got tangled in his head. For a moment he was back on the road with his dad's car.

"Borrowed without permission" was what went down in the report. Steve had no idea the day would end like this; he certainly never intended it to.

It all started late that afternoon. His dad was still asleep, trying to get over a flu that had kicked him in the gut— and kept him down. Steve was bored and knew Dad might be out for hours. And he was dying to try it out.

Steve tiptoed to the kitchen counter and plucked the bundle of keys . . . just to look them over. There was a new one there—the key to unlocking a just-purchased, reconditioned MG, a "bug-eye." Stealing a look through the front window, Steve couldn't help whispering, "Wow—it's perfect!" Bright white, it gleamed in the sunshine. And it had such power. Steve was in love. . . .

He had to take her around the block. He wouldn't even be gone long enough for Dad to know he was gone. If he was awake, Steve was sure he'd have said, "Go ahead, take her for a drive." Anyway, it wasn't worth the risk of hearing no for an answer. So he'd go ahead and take it and be back before anyone knew he was gone.

But things didn't work out quite the way he planned. The "mint"-condition antique developed a nasty hack, and Steve had to pull the wheel hard to try to get it to respond. He rolled the knocking, sputtering bulk into a nearby gas station and tried for some free advice, which was about all he could afford. Turned out that the "bug-eye" just needed a little tweak under the hood, and the mechanic, who was admiring the engine, went ahead and fixed it for nothing. On the house!

What a relief. . . .

Steve took off down the road, checking out the interstate to see how it would handle. It flowed—and flew! It was unreal! Steve was ecstatic until he noticed (too late) the needle on that little red *E.* Empty!

A few pings, and it was all over. Miles from town, barely on the shoulder, and no fuel.

Great, he thought. After thirty minutes of waiting a highway patrol cruiser swung in behind him and gave him a complimentary gallon or so. Steve couldn't thank him enough. He said he'd fill it up at the next station—and he did. Two lucky escapes in the face of trouble. He knew he shouldn't push his luck.

Besides, he'd been gone almost two hours! His dad was probably getting worried—and real sore at him.

Steve thought about calling home but decided it'd be best to just make a beeline for the house and explain it all there. Maybe he was going too fast; maybe it wasn't his fault. Funny, it doesn't really matter. He swerved to avoid the red blur that pulled out in front of him and found himself skidding as the "bug-eye" slammed into this obstacle that appeared out of nowhere. It felt as if twenty huge cymbals smashed in his head.

Steve's eyes closed. He slept during the wild ride to the hospital. His last thought was, *What will Dad say?*

Is it ever too late?

Can abstinence "from this day forward" be a real option if you've already gone past the point of no return? If you've already been sexually active, what can you do?

First, know this: It's never too late to make a fresh start. Never!

Whether it's happened one time or a dozen or more times, you're not a virgin anymore. That's a fact. Considering the statistics we've already given you, odds are pretty good that many of the young people reading this book are in that category. Once you've had sex, you can't go back. Right?

Wrong! You *can* make a change!

Yeah, it may be like tasting ice cream once and never having it again. You've got to recognize that the craving might be enormous. You remember how it tasted, how much you may have enjoyed it. So who's going to stop with just one taste? Besides, if you've already had sex, there's the chance you've already picked up an STD or even HIV. So why stop when it's too late?

"Secondary virginity" applies to me because I realized that just having sex did not make me a man. —Tom Sirotnick, former USC lineman

---

Because it's never too late to do the right thing. There is a new movement taking place in our nation, and it's giving people who have been sexually active a new perspective on the past, the present, and the future. People who have thought the future was pretty well set because of the choices they made in the past are discovering a wonderful thing: You *can* start over.

Have you ever seen a stained-glass window in a home or church? They're beautiful, aren't they? And what's incredible is that they are made out of a bunch of pieces of broken glass. Little chips of crushed, seemingly useless, colored glass are gathered together, set in place, and fitted to form wonderful scenes of flowers, landscapes, or other beautiful images of life. It requires a real artist to take something shattered and broken and create beauty from it.

There's an Artist like that who can take broken and shattered lives, those that have been damaged by premarital sexual activity, and put them back together again to become something wonderful. I'm talking about Christ—and no, I'm not ashamed to mention him and the ways he can help us. If you're not used to this kind of discussion, bear with me for the next few paragraphs while I mention an option that provides real hope.

It's true you won't necessarily escape the results of the life you've led to this point, but you can walk away clean inside, knowing your future can be as beautiful and pure as you decide it will be.

I won't kid you. Becoming a virgin again is impossible from the physical standpoint. But it's entirely possible from a spiritual standpoint. You can go through a transformation and come out right— with yourself and, more important—with God.

In the Bible, God tells us that if we confess our sins—not just sexual sins but all sins, the things we've done wrong—he will forgive us. If we go to God and tell him what we've done, accepting responsibility for our actions and decisions, then ask him to forgive us, he will! In 1 John 1:9, the Bible says: "If we confess our sins, He is faithful and righteous to forgive us our sins and to cleanse us from all unrighteousness."

As far as God is concerned, when you ask him to forgive you, the wrong is ended. It's cleaned up. Gone. You don't have to feel guilty about it anymore because in God's mind it no longer exists.

But how can God forgive my sins? Because of what his Son, Jesus, did on the cross. The Bible also tells us: "He Himself bore our sins in His body on the cross, that we might die to sin and live to righteousness; for by His wounds you were healed" (1 Peter 2:24).

You see, when Christ died on the cross,

he took the punishment for all your sins, all my sins, the whole world's sin. That means you can walk away clean, in right standing with God. "But don't I have to do anything?" you might ask. Well, there is one thing. God offers you forgiveness through Christ as a free gift. You don't have to earn it. You just have to realize your need for it and accept it. John 3:16 says: "For God so loved the world [that includes you], that He gave His only begotten Son, that whoever believes in Him should not perish, but have eternal life."

You must simply believe that the forgiveness that God has provided in Christ is sufficient to make you right with God. And it is, believe me. I have *never* regretted giving my life to Christ and allowing him to make something beautiful out of those broken pieces.

Of course, there may still be struggles with guilt and shame. You'll probably have to deal with the consequences of what you did. But you won't be facing those things alone. The God of the Bible, the God who made you and loves you, will be there with you, helping you. For as long as it takes.

Once you've been forgiven, everything is new again. Everything. And you can start your life over, making right decisions. Decisions that are best for you. It won't be easy. It is never easy to say no to something you've said yes to in the past. Especially something that seems as natural as sex. But you can do it. Take a lesson from millions of others all over the nation who have made the same decision.

Groups of kids—both those who are virgins and those who have been sexually active in the past but have decided to say no from now until their wedding day—have chosen abstinence as their response to the deafening message: You must have sex!

When you decide to choose abstinence, check with churches in your area for a support group. If you can't find one, talk with a youth group leader, your parents, pastor, or teacher about where you might find help and support. See appendix B at the end of this book for organizations that can offer you help in sticking to your decision.

But once you make the decision for abstinence, you have to make some

changes in the way you act and think.
Abstinence isn't easy, but what of any real
value *is* easy? You have to prepare yourself for the battles to come. And they're
out there!

**It's easier to say no than you
think it is. —Sherise**

To recap, remember that if you've been
sexually active, you have some challenges
to face. It won't be easy, but you can do it.
These five steps will help.

Step One: Remember why you're start-
ing over. First and foremost, remind yourself that you can have a completely fresh
start. Wipe the chalkboard clean. Then
remind yourself why you decided abstinence was the right choice for you. Keep
those reasons clear in your mind. You may
want to write them down to help you
remember them. It will make it feel more
"official." Why do you think people write
out business contracts or important agree-
ments? Because things are more powerful
and binding when they are in writing.

Write out a contract with yourself promising to stay sexually pure.

Step Two: Take a hard, honest look at your relationships. Where do you need to make changes? Do you need to clean up what you're thinking or what you watch or read? For example, did you get into a sexual relationship because you were feeling lonely or because it seemed like nobody cared that you were alive? If so, you are in a very dangerous cycle—using sex to get love. Trust me, it doesn't work. Maybe you should start reaching out to others who feel unloved instead. Sometimes giving to others brings us the very thing we need.

Martin, a fifteen-year-old high school student, found this to be true. When he and his girlfriend started dating, it was the first time he'd felt special, like he mattered. Then they started having sex, which seemed OK—until she dumped him. Good-bye—get out of here—leave me alone. He felt more rejected than ever! After talking with some friends, he realized sex wasn't the answer to his feelings. So he started doing some work in an animal shelter to get his mind off his ex-girlfriend.

Before long he joined a program where volunteers from the shelter took dogs to a nursing home. "It felt great!" he said. "These old people would be sitting there, looking all depressed, until we came in with the dogs. Then their faces would get all full of smiles! It was like we were the most important people in the world! They loved the dogs, and the dogs got a kick out of all the attention. It made me feel like I was doing something important." Martin poured his energy into positive activities. That is very important.

Step Three: Ask for supernatural help. No matter how strong you may be, you won't be able to do this on your own. None of the temptations and pressures that caused you to experiment with sex are going to disappear. You need help. So go ahead and ask. God will give you the strength and determination needed to keep your commitment if you ask him.

Step Four: Find someone you can trust to talk to. It's always helpful to have a sounding board—your own personal think tank—someone you can tell what's happening and what you're thinking. Find someone who believes in and practices (or practiced before they were married) abstinence. A youth leader, a pastor, an older sister or brother, or even your parents—someone who understands the struggle. It would be great if you could get together to talk and pray on a regular basis—not just when you're in trouble, but as friends. Keep those lines of communication open.

Step Five: Be willing to admit you're tempted—or when you fail. And everyone does fail at times. The important thing is not to try to hide it and pretend you're doing fine, that there's nothing wrong. Talk about your feelings with a same-sex friend who will encourage you and hold you accountable to your commitment.

No matter what you've done to this point, you can start over today! Commit yourself to abstinence—and follow the suggestions outlined in the next chapter.

In the hospital bed, Steve looked up into his dad's brown eyes. A cheap hospital curtain partitioned off the two of them from the noise and scurrying in the ER recovery room. His father had been waiting there for Steve to come out of it. As they looked at each other, no words would come.

Deep down, Steve knew he didn't have to worry because his father loved him, and still did, even though he had made a big mistake. He had definitely blown it, but his dad forgave him anyway.

But he also held him accountable. Steve was the one who had to work all summer to make repairs on the "bug-eye," missing out on lots of other things he'd rather have been doing. But he paid his debt.

It was simply the cost of his behavior. And such costs should be considered well in advance. One day, sooner or later, the bill must be paid.

How painful the repayment plan must be—and how much we must sacrifice in the process—is determined by how wisely we consider the consequences before we act.

THINK ABOUT IT

1. Why can you be proud to be a virgin—even a "second-chance" virgin?

2. Even if you have made mistakes in the past, isn't it better to make a clean start than to make matters worse by continuing dangerous behavior? Why or why not?

3. Why would it be helpful to hang around others who have made the abstinence choice?

9
Just Say No

WHILE you may have heard much about "safe sex" and the other issues we've addressed so far, abstinence may be a new concept for you. Believe it or not, many high school students haven't even heard of it before. And those who have might not be too sure about its meaning.

Abstinence means waiting until marriage for sex.

That may seem like an impossible goal. Or maybe you think that the suggestion to wait somehow implies that I think sex is bad. No way! When you understand how special and wonderful sex can be—

and how powerful and important as
well—you'll start looking at it differently.
With some respect—even awe. We discussed this at the end of chapter 1, and it
is very important to understand.

Those who wait until marriage to have
sex recognize that it can be a source of
great joy. In fact, as we saw, the research
shows that those who wait until marriage
enjoy better sex than those who don't.
Yet, handled carelessly and thoughtlessly,
it can bring you disappointment, pain, disease, and disaster. Sex is something far too
great to give away to just anyone, too
potent to play with—and definitely not
worth dying for.

Abstinence involves making an
informed decision—your own decision.

You can choose to abstain. When it
comes right down to it, having sex before
marriage very seldom gives people what
they're looking for: a sense of being loved
and belonging. Instead, something that's a
precious gift—sharing ourselves in the
most intimate way possible—is made
about as special as a free sample of snack
cakes they hand out in the grocery store!

More than ten years ago Michael Jackson wrote a song that said: "Bodies on bodies, like sacks upon shelves/People just using each other to make love to themselves." That's exactly what sex has become for many people. A way to make themselves feel good. They aren't looking for ways to please out of love and concern for their partner. They're just looking for the immediate sensual experience. It's selfish.

Sex can and should generate a powerful bond, a relational superglue between two people. In the setting of a permanent and public commitment (marriage), sex can be savored, explored, and nurtured without guilt or fear.

Think about it. Imagine how incredible sex could be when it is based on acceptance and true love rather than performance and pressure. "If you really loved me, you'd do it" would never come into play. Think about having sex without fear of rejection. Pleasing and encouraging your partner become the primary agenda. As difficult as it may seem, abstinence can work. And it can work well. It can set you free from the many pressures of sex. And it can give you a without-a-doubt guarantee—and a real promise. As you consider choosing abstinence, keep one other thought in mind: Having sex isn't like breathing—you can live without it.

There are some interesting myths going around today that are pretty insulting both to teens and their sense of integrity and responsibility. The lines go like this:

- Teens won't listen to the abstinence message.
- Having sex is inevitable for young people.
- If you're not having sex, something is wrong with you.

But it's the people saying these things who are wrong—dead wrong.

Here is one place where the statistics actually reflect good news because one study done by the U.S. Department of Health and Human Services showed that almost 65 percent of all high school females under eighteen are virgins![1] In addition, when a group of teens were asked what they wanted most from a sex-education program, 84 percent indicated they wanted information on "how to say 'no' without hurting the other person's feelings." [2] Somebody's interested in abstinence.

And lots of teens are listening to the message.

A December 1991 *USA Today* poll called chastity the "second sexual revolution." That poll showed that more than half of all adults (54 percent) and two-thirds of teenagers (63 percent) find the so-called safe-sex message disturbing because it implies an endorsement of casual sex. In other words, sex in such cases is seen as cheap, dirty, and meaningless. The poll also showed that the majority of adults and teens agreed that today's adolescents don't hear enough about saying no to sex. [3]

Are you in the minority if you choose abstinence? Not likely.

More and more people are getting the idea. Abstinence works where "safe sex" is failing. The January 16, 1994, issue of the *New York Times* featured an article on the front page that was entitled "Sex Educators for Young See New Virtue in Chastity." In the article, Lori, a fourteen-year-old girl, was shown learning how to say no to sex and how to develop strategies that would save her virginity. Her teacher played the role of would-be seducer, testing Lori with crude comments and sweet promises. Lori looked her teacher straight in the eyes and answered him: "No." No excuses. No explanations. Just no.

The article goes on to say,

> Lori is one of a growing number of teenagers around the country, 180,000 . . . in California, who are learning the rewards of postponing sex. In classrooms, community centers and church basements, these young people . . . are being encouraged to resist the messages of rap lyrics and the bullying of their peers and to prepare for success rather than settle for pregnancy and poverty.

Programs that emphasize abstinence instead of "safe sex" are finding new acceptance from lots of family-planning experts. Because of the epidemic of teen pregnancy and the growing rates of AIDS

among teens, chastity is making a come-
back. Finally.

**I hear a lot more of "Cool,
you're a virgin," you know.
It's a lot more positive than
it used to be. —Alison**

One recent report said that in Mary-
land it's virtually impossible to drive the
highways or ride the buses without seeing posters that say "Abstinence makes
the heart grow fonder" or billboards trum-
peting that virginity is "Not a Dirty Word."
State officials say the messages, part of a
$5-million advertising campaign, are
responsible for reducing teenage pregnancy by more than 10 percent in two
years.[4]

Wait a minute! Back up! The abstinence
message is reducing teen pregnancy . . .
and disease . . . and death . . . and heart-
ache. . . . So I leave it up to you. Is abstinence a good choice or not?

It is not only the wise path to travel. It
is also becoming quite popular.

HOW TO SAY NO

Let's look at some simple steps to help you "just say no." Go ahead, take a deep breath, and let's hit the final stretch running!

1. Decide ahead of time that sex begins on the wedding night and not before. When you have a decision already formed in your mind, you don't have to worry about the circumstances, the suggestive conversations, or anything else that might sway you from what you've decided. Nothing will happen to change your mind when you know what you want and are willing to stick with it.

Believe it or not, this can make dating a lot easier and a lot more fun. You don't have to waste your time wondering whether or not your date will expect anything from you—or if you'll give in. You already know what won't be happening, so you can relax and enjoy your time together. And, if your date pushes you to change your mind or doesn't agree with your decision, no problem! Tell them how it is and send them on their way.

And don't go out with that person again.

That's a crucial point.

No matter how much you may like that guy or girl, it's vital that they understand and respect who you are. If they can't do that, it's a pretty good sign that they don't care about you. And backing down on your decision won't make them change their minds. After all, if you're not treating yourself with respect, there's no reason why anyone else will either. The other good reason to stay away from someone who tries to force you into doing something you don't want to do is the fact that "next time" you might not be able to handle the temptation as well as you did this time! Nothing too tricky here—simple common sense.

Remember, you are a valuable, important person, and you deserve—and should demand—respect. Don't settle for anything less.

2. Know your reasons. Know why you have made the decision to wait. Write your reasons down, and keep them where they can serve as a reminder. Here

are a few thoughts other teens have listed.
They might help get you started.

- I want to enjoy sex fully and
  freely—in marriage—where it is
  part of a committed relationship.
- I don't want to risk getting a serious disease.
- I don't want to get pregnant.
- Who needs a relationship based on
  sex?
- It's what God says is right and best.
- The chance for an education can
  pass me by.
- I want to make something of my
  life.
- You can't support a baby on lunch
  money!
- There are better ways to be a real
  man (or woman).

Whatever your reasons, keep them
clearly in mind (and keep your mind
clear, too). Carry your written reasons
with you if you need to. If someone starts
pressuring you, pull your reasons out and
hand them over. Sometimes people need

to see it in black and white to get the message that you're serious.

3. Avoid situations that increase the risk of a sexual encounter. A group of girls who were living in a home for unwed mothers got together and wrote letters. Their topic: My Message to Teenagers. Their experiences weren't all the same, but each had learned some common lessons:

"Think before you act."

"Don't let one night of passion cause you a lifetime of regret."

"Don't get into a situation where you know you'll be tempted."

Remember, it's a whole lot easier to apply the brakes before you start rolling down the hill out of control!

4. Stay sober. Alcohol and drugs cloud judgment and weaken resolve. Don't let them.

5. Don't be a sucker for a clever come-on. There is no limit to a person's imagination and creativity, especially when it comes to getting something they really want. And when someone wants sex (and

wants it real bad), you never know what
will come out of their mouth.

It might help to write down some of
the lines you've heard and come up with
responses. You and your friends may even
want to do this together and help each
other out. You'll also have a good laugh
over the tired old lines people still use.
Or at least try to use!

Just to help get you started, here are
some examples:

LINE: Sex will make our relationship
    better.
RESPONSE: No, it won't. It will become
    the center of attention and choke out
    everything else.

LINE: Sex will bring us closer.
RESPONSE: It will only bring our bodies
    closer. But it can drive the rest of us apart.

LINE: Don't you love me?
RESPONSE: Don't you respect me?

LINE: If you love me, you'll let me.
RESPONSE: If you love me, you won't ask
    me.

LINE: It's our anniversary. It's special.
RESPONSE: It will be even more special if we wait for our wedding night.

LINE: I want to give you something to remember me by.
RESPONSE: Like a baby or a disease?

LINE: If you won't, I'll find someone who will.
RESPONSE: I hope the two of you have a very nice life together.

LINE: What are you, scared?
RESPONSE: Of HIV or getting pregnant? Who wouldn't be?

LINE: Don't be so uptight.
RESPONSE: Don't be so selfish!

LINE: Don't worry. I've got protection.
RESPONSE: So do I. It's called saying no. And my protection is 100 percent safe.

THE CHOICE IS YOURS

Sex is everywhere. I know that. You know that. There's no getting away from the message that casual sex is OK. But you

can limit your exposure, and you don't
have to buy it. Not for a second.

You can be sure, no matter where you
live, that you'll be faced with sexual temptations at some point. So be ready.

And believe it or not, you should enjoy
sex!

But in the right place, at the right time,
with the right person. I want you to discover the wonder and enjoyment of sex
that is experienced in a loving, committed, exclusive relationship—and that
doesn't start until you say "I do!" I want
you to know the joy of exploring your
sexuality with confidence and security
because you're sharing it with your marriage partner, a person to whom you will
be faithful for life.

To do that, you'll need to choose abstinence long before the sexual temptation
comes knocking at your emotional door.
Or, if you've already said yes to sex, you
need to decide it's not worth the risk.
And you can.

But, bottom line, it's your call. You have
to decide what you will do, and with the
information we have discussed, choosing
abstinence is clearly the intelligent

choice. Don't let a pushy girlfriend or boyfriend (or the crowd) make important decisions for you that could affect the rest of your life. Stand for what you believe, protect your dignity, and enjoy your young life.

THINK ABOUT IT

1. Are you insulted by those who say teenagers do not have enough self-control to refrain from sex?

2. Even if abstinence weren't becoming a more popular option, why would it be the best route to take?

3. Do you think dating would be more fun without the pressure to have sex?

4. What are some of the lines you've heard to pressure someone into sex? How would you respond?

Appendix A: Adoption Resources

EXODUS 2:1-10 tells the story of Pharaoh's daughter discovering the infant Moses at the river and later adopting him as her son. Families today, particularly infertile couples, may experience the same joy and satisfaction through the positive alternative of adoption.

This appendix lists organizations that provide assistance to those who are interested in adopting a child or giving one up for adoption. Also listed is some Canadian adoption information.

Please note that all organizations included in this appendix are listed for

your information only, that they are not
necessarily Christian in their approach,
and that their listing in this publication
does not in any way constitute an
endorsement by Focus on the Family. We
strongly suggest that you personally contact each organization to evaluate its information and/or programs prior to initiating
any personal involvement with them.

U.S. ADOPTION RESOURCES

Academy of California Adoption Lawyers

Will provide a free brochure upon
request.

Academy of California Adoption
  Lawyers
926 Garden Street
Santa Barbara, CA 93101
(805) 962-0988

Adoptive Families of America

Serves parents who have adopted or who
are waiting to adopt children from all
countries. They are a national umbrella
organization for over 300 adoptive parent
support groups. A help line is available 24

hours a day for families in crisis. They do
not discuss adoption in general, but they
can provide information about adoption
issues, health insurance, equity, and adoption procedures. A free general information booklet for prospective adoptive
parents is available through this organization. They also publish a bimonthly magazine called *Adoptive Families.*

Adoptive Families of America
3333 Highway 100 North
Minneapolis, MN 55422
(612) 535-4829
(612) 535-7808 (FAX)

Bethany Christian Services

One of the largest private adoption agencies in the country, with 57 offices in 28
states. Their services include pro-life pregnancy counseling, temporary foster care,
infant foster-care placement, alternative
living arrangements for pregnant women,
shepherding homes, and international
adoptions.

Bethany Christian Services
901 Eastern Avenue NE

Grand Rapids, MI 49503
(616) 459-6273 (main office)
(310) 804-3448 (Bellflower office/Los
   Angeles County)
(800) 238-4269 (hot line staffed with
   volunteers)

The offices in Grand Rapids, Michigan,
and Bellflower, California, have Spanish-
speaking counselors. Spanish literature is
available directly from

Bethany Christian Services
9928 Flower, Suite 202
Bellflower, CA 90706

Christian Family Care Agency

C.F.C.A. serves families in crisis through
counseling, pregnancy assistance, foster
care, and adoption. Video and slide presenta-
tions, speakers, and brochures are available
upon request. They publish a semiannual
newsletter called *CFCA Update*.

Christian Family Care Agency
3603 North Seventh Avenue
Phoenix, AZ 85013
(602) 234-1935

The National Adoption Center
A telecommunication network that connects agencies around the country, allowing prospective families and special-needs children to be registered and matched.

> The National Adoption Center
> 1500 Walnut Street, Suite 701
> Philadelphia, PA 19102
> (800) TO-ADOPT (862-3678)
> (215) 735-9988

The National Council for Adoption
This council publishes the *Adoption Factbook* ($48 including shipping and handling). It is a summary of state adoption regulations, adoption statistics, current adoption issues, financial considerations, and adoption resources.

> The National Council for Adoption
> 1930 Seventeenth Street NW
> Washington, D.C. 20009
> (202) 328-1200

ADOPTION SEARCH ORGANIZATIONS
The following organizations offer help in locating birth parents or children. Both

parents and children must be registered
with the organization in order to find
each other. Please note that the disclaimer given at the start of this appendix
applies to the organizations listed below.

Concerned United Birth Parents
    Janet Fenton, President
    2000 Walker Street
    Des Moines, IA 50317
    (515) 263-9541

**International Soundex Reunion
Registry**
Offers an extensive referral list.

    International Soundex Reunion Registry
    P.O. Box 2312
    Carson City, NV 89702
    (702) 882-7755

Pure Inc.
    P.O. Box 638
    Westminster, CA 92684
    (714) 892-4098

CANADIAN ADOPTION RESOURCES
Please note that the disclaimer given at

the start of this appendix applies to the organizations listed below.

Alliance for Life
This is an umbrella organization that can provide information on specific agencies across Canada.

Alliance for Life
B1-90 Garry Street
Winnipeg, MB R3C 4H1
(204) 942-4772

Jewels for Jesus Mission and Adoption Agency
This organization serves Ontario, Canada, with a crisis pregnancy service and an adoption agency.

Jewels for Jesus Mission and Adoption
   Agency
6981 Mill Creek Drive, Unit 22
Mississauga, ON L5N 6B8
(905) 821-7494

Appendix B: Recommended Abstinence Organizations

THERE are a number of organizations that are doing excellent and effective work in helping adolescents abstain from sexual activity. Some provide educational resources for schools; others will provide guest speakers to groups. A few offer videos and printed materials that are helpful. There are also medical organizations that provide solid information on matters of sexuality.

ORGANIZATIONS PROVIDING EDUCATIONAL MATERIALS FOR SCHOOLS

Teen Aid
Targeted for junior- and senior-high levels. Teen Aid has a very good HIV course as well as a character-based sex-education program. It has been piloted in a number of schools and is a national program.

Teen Aid
723 E. Jackson
Spokane, WA 99207
(509) 482-2868

Teen Choice
This is a character-based/abstinence education program that is comprehensive in nature and well written for school use.

Teen Choice
Martha Long
6201 Leesburg Pike, Suite 404
Falls Church, VA 22044
(703) 532-9455

Responsible Sexual Values Program (RSVP)

Targeted for grades K–5, with a program also for 6th–9th grades.

> Responsible Sexual Values Program
> 6434 East Main Street
> Reynoldsburg, OH 43068
> (614) 864-7787

Best Friends

This is an excellent mentoring project that helps teens resist many types of negative behaviors: sex, drugs, gangs, etc. It is "mentoring" because peers and counselors help teens say no to the pressure to engage in negative behavior. Best Friends can only be as successful as the commitment level of the school guidance area or in terms of strong mentors to help make the project succeed.

> Best Friends
> Elayne Bennett
> Georgetown University
> Child Development Center
> 2233 Wisconsin Avenue NW, Suite 215
> Washington, D.C. 20007

(202) 338-1122
(301) 907-9003

The Loving Well Project

This is a character/values-based curriculum that was developed by the College of Communication and the School of Education at Boston University. It is unique in its approach since it is a literature-based program that addresses the value of abstinence and commitment through various forms of literature. This program was federally funded by the U.S. Department of Health and Human Services in the past.

> The Loving Well Project
> The School of Education
> Boston University
> Nancy McClaren, Project Coordinator
> 605 Commonwealth Avenue
> Boston, MA 02215
> (617) 353-4088

Choosing the Best

Choosing the Best is being piloted in fifty Illinois schools.

> Choosing the Best
> Project Reality

Kathleen Sullivan
P.O. Box 97
Gulf, IL 60029-0097
(708) 729-3308

Family Accountability Communicating Teen Sexuality (FACTS)

An abstinence program with a strong component of parental involvement.

Family Accountability Communicating
  Teen Sexuality
Northeast Family Services
Rose Fuller, Director
4805 NE Glisan Street
Portland, OR 97213
(503) 230-6377

Focus on the Family

Focus on the Family distributes the thirty-minute video *Sex, Lies, & . . . the Truth,* which reveals the hard truth about sex in the '90s. It is available in both public school and Christian versions. Focus has also prepared an excellent educational curriculum by the same name for classroom or group instruction.

Focus on the Family
P.O. Box 35500
Colorado Springs, CO 80935-3550
(800) A-FAMILY (232-6459)

ORGANIZATIONS CONDUCTING ON-CAMPUS ABSTINENCE PROGRAMS

Summer Night Communications
John Harris lectures extensively on high school and college campuses throughout the country on HIV/STDs and condom effectiveness.

Summer Night Communications
John Harris
P.O. Box 28130
Fresno, CA 93729
(209) 431-6837

Choices
Priscilla Hurley, Director
P.O. Box 2124
Yorba Linda, CA 92686
(714) 524-1236

Sex, Love and Choices
Right to Live League of Southern
    California

Gwen Shaw
1028 N. Lake Avenue
Pasadena, CA 91104
(818) 398-6100

Athletes for Abstinence
A. C. Green
1015 Gayley Avenue, Suite 1031
Los Angeles, CA 90024
(310) 670-9766

MEDICAL ORGANIZATIONS PROVIDING INFORMATION ON HIV/STD PREVENTION

Medical Institute for Sexual Health (MISH)

MISH is a medical information organization that compiles and disseminates data on sexually transmitted diseases and condom efficacy.

Medical Institute for Sexual Health
Joseph S. McIlhaney, Jr., M.D.
P.O. Box 4919
Austin, TX 78765
(800) 892-9484

Americans for a Sound AIDS Policy (ASAP)

ASAP seeks a responsible approach to stemming the HIV/AIDS epidemic.

Americans for a Sound AIDS Policy
Shepard Smith
P.O. Box 17433
Washington, D.C. 20041

National Institute for Healthcare Research (NIHR)

NIHR conducts and publishes research concerning health care issues.

National Institute for Healthcare
    Research
David Larson, M.D., M.S.P.H.
6110 Executive Boulevard, Suite 680
Rockville, MD 20852
(301) 984-7162

Notes

Chapter 1

1. Alan Guttmacher Institute, "Sexually Transmitted Diseases in the United States," *Facts in Brief* (New York, September 1993), 1.

2. Robert T. Michael, John H. Gagnon, and Edward O. Lauman, *Sex in America: A Definitive Survey* (Boston: Little, Brown and Co., 1994), 124.

3. Ibid., 125.

4. Ibid.

5. "Redbook Survey on Female Sexuality," *Redbook* 145, September 1975, 54.

6. Kari Jenson Gold, "Getting Real," *First Things,* January 1994, 6.

Chapter 2

1. Richard Gordon, "A Critical Review of the Physics and Statistics of Condoms and Their Role in Individual versus Societal Survival of the AIDS Epidemic," *Journal of Sex & Marital Therapy* 15, no. 1 (spring 1989): 5–29.

Chapter 3

1. Mitch McConnell, "Hit Porn Purveyors Where It

Hurts: Link to Violence Could Be Shown," *St. Louis Post-Dispatch,* 26 August 1991, 3B.

2. Tom Minnery, ed., *Pornography: A Human Tragedy* (Wheaton, Ill.: Tyndale, 1986), 125.

Chapter 4

1. "Teen Births: Formula for Disaster," *USA Today,* 22 February 1994, 1A.

2. Centers for Disease Control (CDC), "Sexual Behavior among High School Students—United States, 1990," *Morbidity and Mortality Weekly Report* 40, no. 51 & 52, 1.

3. Bureau of the Census, *Statistical Abstract of the United States: 1993* (Washington, D.C., 1993), 83.

4. David Blankenhorn, *Fatherless America* (New York: Basic Books, 1995), 1, 22.

5. Ronald F. Carey, et al., "Effectiveness of Latex Condoms as a Barrier to Human Immunodeficiency Virus–Sized Particles under Conditions of Simulated Use," *Sexually Transmitted Diseases* 19 (July/August 1992): 230–34.

6. Gregory B. Davis and L. W. Schroeder, "Influence of Contact Angles on the Leakage of Latex Condoms," *Journal of Testing and Evaluation* 18, no. 5 (September 1990): 352–58.

7. Carey, "Latex Condoms," 233.

8. University of Texas Medical Branch at Galveston, *UTMB News,* 7 June 1993, quoting Susan C. Weller, "A Meta-Analysis of Condom Effectiveness in

Reducing Sexually Transmitted HIV," *Social Science & Medicine* 36, no. 36 (June 1993): 1635–44.

9. Richard Gordon, "A Critical Review of the Physics and Statistics of Condoms and Their Role in Individual versus Societal Survival of the AIDS Epidemic," *Journal of Sex & Marital Therapy* 15, no. 1 (spring 1989): 5–29.

10. E. F. Jones and J. D. Forrest, "Contraceptive Failure Rates Based on the 1988 NSFG," *Family Planning Perspectives* (January/February 1992): 12–19.

11. "Condom Effectiveness Study in Los Angeles Loses Funding," *Washington Post,* 10 August 1988.

12. Craig Carmichael, "Concerted Effort: One Student's Stand on Sex Education Policy," *Outlook,* spring 1994, 26.

13. CDC, "Sexual Behavior."

14. Kenneth L. Noller, *OB/GYN Clinical Alert,* September 1992.

15. Theresa Crenshaw, from remarks made at the National Conference on HIV, Washington, D.C., November 15–18, 1991.

16. Adolescent enrollment in only *one* federal program—Title X—from 1970 to 1992 totaled more than $1 billion.

17. Isabelle de Vincenzi, "Comparison of Female to Male and Male to Female Transmission of HIV in 563 Stable Couples," *British Medical Journal* 304 (March 1992): 809–13; Alberto Saracco, et al., "Man-to-Woman Sexual Transmission of HIV: Longitudinal

Study of 343 Steady Partners of Infected Men," *Journal of Acquired Immune Deficiency Syndromes* 6, no. 5 (1993): 497–502.

18. Dr. Isabelle de Vincenzi, telephone conversation with Mike Ebert, 17 February 1994.

19. "Most Adults in the United States Who Have Multiple Sexual Partners Do Not Use Condoms Consistently," *Family Planning Perspectives* (January/February 1994): 42–43.

20. "Condom Campaign Fails to Increase Sales," *Wall Street Journal,* 23 July 94.

21. Gordon, "Critical Review of Condoms," 5–29.

22. "As Adolescent Males Age, Risky Behavior Rises but Condom Use Decreases," *Family Planning Perspectives* (January/February 1994): 45–46.

23. Marion Howard and Judith Blamey McCabe, "Helping Teens Postpone Sexual Involvement," *Family Planning Perspectives* 22, no. 1 (1990): 21–26.

24. Barbara Dafoe Whitehead, "The Failure of Sex Education," *Atlantic Monthly,* October 1994, 68.

Chapter 5

1. "Birthrate Soars at Colorado School," *USA Today,* 19 May 1992.

2. Douglas Kirby, "School-Based Programs to Reduce Sexual Risk-Taking Behaviors: Sexuality and HIV/AIDS Education, Health Clinics and Condom Availability Programs" (manuscript submitted to *Public Health Reports,* 15 January 1994), 24.

3. Centers for Disease Control (CDC), *Condoms and Their Use in Preventing HIV Infection and Other STDs* (Atlanta, 30 July 1993).

4. "Update: Barrier Protection against HIV Infection and Other Sexually Transmitted Diseases," *Morbidity and Mortality Weekly Report* 42, no. 30 (6 August 1993). This also appeared in *Journal of the American Medical Association* 270, no. 8 (25 August 1993): 933–34.

5. CDC, *Condoms and Their Use,* 1.

6. Food and Drug Administration, Center for Devices and Radiological Health, *Condoms and Sexually Transmitted Diseases, Especially AIDS* (Health and Human Services publication 90–4239, Washington, D.C., 1992).

7. "Research Reveals Condom Conundrum," *Journal of NIH Research* 5 (January 1993): 32–33.

8. Centers for Disease Control (CDC), "Sexual Behavior among High School Students—United States, 1990," *Morbidity and Mortality Weekly Report* 40, no. 51 & 52, 1.

9. "As Adolescent Males Age, Risky Behavior Rises but Condom Use Decreases," *Family Planning Perspectives* (January/February 1994): 45–46.

10. Ronald F. Carey, et al., "Effectiveness of Latex Condoms as a Barrier to Human Immunodeficiency Virus–Sized Particles under Conditions of Simulated Use," *Sexually Transmitted Diseases* 19 (July/August 1992): 230–34; University of Texas Medical Branch at Galveston, *UTMB News,* 7 June 1993, quoting Susan C. Weller, "A Meta-Analysis of Condom Effec-

tiveness in Reducing Sexually Transmitted HIV," *Social Science & Medicine* 36, no. 36 (June 1993): 1635–44.

11. Joseph S. McIlhaney, Jr., M.D., *1250 Health-Care Questions Women Ask* (Grand Rapids: Baker, 1992), 751.

12. *Family Practice News,* 15 December 1977, cited in James H. Ford and Michael Schwartz, "Birth Control for Teenagers: Diagram for Disaster," *Linacre Quarterly,* February 1979, 76.

Chapter 6

1. Kenneth L. Noller, *OB/GYN Clinical Alert,* September 1992.

2. Robert Reid, M.D., *American College of Obstetricians and Gynecologists Newsletter,* August 1989.

3. David Blankenhorn, *Fatherless America* (New York: Basic Books, 1995), 1.

4. Glenn T. Stanton, "Twice As Strong: The Undeniable Advantage of Raising Children in a Traditional Two-Parent Family," (research paper for Focus on the Family, 1995. Request item #FC033).

5. Bureau of the Census, *Statistical Abstract of the United States: 1993* (Washington, D.C., 1993), 83.

6. Vincent M. Rue, "The Psychological Realities of Induced Abortion," in Michael T. Mannion, ed., *Post-Abortion Aftermath: A Comprehensive Consideration* (Kansas City, Mo.: Sheed & Ward, 1994), 17.

7. Ibid., 18.

8. Ibid.

9. Ibid., 19.

10. Ibid., 24.

11. "Induced Abortion Might Elevate a Woman's Breast Cancer Risk in Later Years," *Family Planning Perspectives* 27, no. 1 (1995): 41–43.

12. Joe S. McIlhaney, Jr., M.D., *1250 Health-Care Questions Women Ask* (Grand Rapids: Baker, 1985), 226.

13. Blankenhorn, *Fatherless America,* 22.

Chapter 7

1. Centers for Disease Control (CDC), *Centers for Disease Control Division of STD/HIV 1991 Annual Report* (Atlanta, 1992), 3.

2. Ibid.

3. Centers for Disease Control (CDC), *Condoms and Their Use in Preventing HIV Infection and Other STDs* (Atlanta, 30 July 1993).

4. Stephen J. Genuis, M.D., "The Dilemma of Adolescent Sexuality; Part 1: The Onslaught of Sexually Transmitted Diseases," *Journal SOGC* 15, no. 5 (June/July 1993): 554.

5. Fernando B. Guijon, M.D., "Co-factors in the Development of Cervical Neoplasia," *The Colposcopist* 26, no. 1 (winter 1994): 1; Barbara Reed, M.D., et al., "Factors Associated with Human Papillomavirus Infection in Women Encountered in Community-Based Offices," *ARCH FAM MED* 2 (December 1993): 1239; Bureau of the Census, *Statistical*

Abstract of the United States: 1993 (Washington, D.C., 1993), 93.

6. Genuis, "Dilemma of Adolescent Sexuality," 554.

7. Ibid., 554–55.

8. Ibid., 556.

9. Ibid.; CDC, *STD/HIV Prevention,* 13.

10. Genuis, "Dilemma of Adolescent Sexuality," 556.

11. Joe S. McIlhaney, Jr., M.D., *1250 Health-Care Questions Women Ask* (Grand Rapids: Baker, 1985), 621–22.

12. Ibid.

13. Alan Guttmacher Institute, "Sexually Transmitted Diseases in the United States," *Facts in Brief* (New York, September 1993), 1.

14. Ibid., 616.

15. Joe S. McIlhaney, Jr., M.D., *Sexuality and Sexually Transmitted Diseases* (Grand Rapids: Baker, 1991), 119.

16. Ibid., 99.

17. Ibid., 108–9.

18. McIlhaney, *1250 Questions,* 613.

19. Ibid., 152.

20. Reed, "Human Papillomavirus Infection," 1239.

21. Bureau of the Census, *Statistical Abstract,* 93.

22. McIlhaney, *Sexuality,* 137.

23. "AIDS Passes Accidents as Leading Killer of Young Adults," Associated Press, 31 January 1995.

24. Ibid.

25. Ibid.

26. Glenn Wood, M.D., and John Dietrich, M.D., *The AIDS Epidemic: Balancing Compassion and Justice* (Portland, Oreg.: Multnomah, 1990), 113–35.

27. Dr. George Lemp, "HIV-1 Seroprevalence and Risk Behaviors among Young Men Who Have Had Sex with Other Men" (unpublished study, San Francisco/Berkeley, 1992–93; distributed by the CDC).

28. Ibid., 122.

29. Jeanne M. Lusher, et al., "Risk of Human Immunodeficiency Virus Type I Infection among Sexual and Nonsexual Household Contacts of Persons with Congenital Clotting Disorders," *Pediatrics* 88, no. 2 (1991): 242.

Chapter 9

1. Centers for Disease Control (CDC), "Percent of Women 15–19 Years of Age Who Are Sexually Experienced, by Race, Age and Marital Status: United States, 1988," in *National Survey of Family Growth* (Washington, D.C., 1988).

2. Marion Howard and Judith Blamey McCabe, "Helping Teenagers Postpone Sexual Involvement," *Family Planning Perspectives* 22, no. 1 (January/February 1990): 21–26.

3. "Sex, Morals, and AIDS," *USA Today Weekend,* 27–29 December 1991, 4.

4. "Sex Educators for Young See New Virtue in Chastity," *New York Times,* 16 January 1994, A13.

Other Living Books Best-sellers

400 CREATIVE WAYS TO SAY I LOVE YOU by Alice Chapin. Perhaps the flame of love has almost died in your marriage, or you have a good marriage that just needs a little spark. Here is a book of creative, practical ideas for the woman who wants to show the man in her life that she cares. 07-0919-5

ANSWERS by Josh McDowell and Don Stewart. In a question-and-answer format, the authors tackle sixty-five of the most-asked questions about the Bible, God, Jesus Christ, miracles, other religions, and Creation. 07-0021-X

BUILDING YOUR SELF-IMAGE by Josh McDowell and Don Stewart. Here are practical answers to help you overcome your fears, anxieties, and lack of self-confidence. Learn how God's higher image of who you are can take root in your heart and mind. 07-1395-8

COME BEFORE WINTER AND SHARE MY HOPE by Charles R. Swindoll. A collection of brief vignettes offering hope and the assurance that adversity and despair are temporary setbacks we can overcome! 07-0477-0

DR. DOBSON ANSWERS YOUR QUESTIONS by Dr. James Dobson. In this convenient reference book, re-nowned author Dr. James Dobson addresses heartfelt concerns on many topics, including questions on marital relationships, infant care, child discipline, home man-agement, and others. 07-0580-7

THE EFFECTIVE FATHER by Gordon MacDonald. A practi-cal study of effective fatherhood based on biblical principles. 07-0669-2

FOR MEN ONLY edited by J. Allan Petersen. This book deals with topics of concern to every man: the business world, marriage, fathering, spiritual goals, and problems of living as a Christian in a secular world. 07-0892-X

FOR WOMEN ONLY by Evelyn R. and J. Allan Petersen. This balanced, entertaining, and diversified treatment covers all the aspects of womanhood. 07-0897-0

GIVERS, TAKERS, AND OTHER KINDS OF LOVERS by Josh McDowell and Paul Lewis. Bypassing generalities about love and sex, this book answers the basics: What-ever happened to sexual freedom? Do men respond differ-ently than women? Here are straight answers about God's plan for love and sexuality. 07-1031-2

Other Living Books Best-sellers

HINDS' FEET ON HIGH PLACES by Hannah Hurnard. A classic allegory of a journey toward faith that has sold more than a million copies! 07-1429-6 *Also on Tyndale Living Audio 15-7426-4*

HOW TO BE HAPPY THOUGH MARRIED by Tim LaHaye. A valuable resource that tells how to develop physical, mental, and spiritual harmony in marriage. 07-1499-7

JOHN, SON OF THUNDER by Ellen Gunderson Traylor. In this saga of adventure, romance, and discovery, travel with John—the disciple whom Jesus loved—down desert paths, through the courts of the Holy City, and to the foot of the cross as he leaves his luxury as a privileged son of Israel for the bitter hardship of his exile on Patmos. 07-1903-4

LET ME BE A WOMAN by Elisabeth Elliot. This best-selling author shares her observations and experiences of male-female relationships in a collection of insightful essays. 07-2162-4

LIFE IS TREMENDOUS! by Charlie "Tremendous" Jones. Believing that enthusiasm makes the difference, Jones shows how anyone can be happy, involved, relevant, productive, healthy, and secure in the midst of a high-pressure, commercialized society. 07-2184-5

MORE THAN A CARPENTER by Josh McDowell. A hard-hitting book for people who are skeptical about Jesus' deity, his resurrection, and his claim on their lives. 07-4552-3 *Also on Tyndale Living Audio 15-7427-2*

QUICK TO LISTEN, SLOW TO SPEAK by Robert E. Fisher. Families are shown how to express love to one another by developing better listening skills, finding ways to disagree without arguing, and using constructive criticism. 07-5111-6

REASONS by Josh McDowell and Don Stewart. In a convenient question-and-answer format, the authors address many of the commonly asked questions about the Bible and evolution. 07-5287-2

THE SECRET OF LOVING by Josh McDowell. McDowell explores the values and qualities that will help both the single and married reader to be the right person for someone else. He offers a fresh perspective for evaluating and improving the reader's love life. 07-5845-5

Other Living Books Best-sellers

THE STORY FROM THE BOOK. From Adam to Armageddon, this book captures the full sweep of the Bible's content in abridged, chronological form. Based on *The Book,* the best-selling, popular edition of *The Living Bible.* 07-6677-6

STRIKE THE ORIGINAL MATCH by Charles Swindoll. Swindoll draws on the best marriage survival guide–the Bible–and his 35 years of marriage to show couples how to survive, flex, grow, forgive, and keep romance alive in their marriage. 07-6445-5

THE STRONG-WILLED CHILD by Dr. James Dobson. Through these practical solutions and humorous anecdotes, parents will learn to discipline an assertive child without breaking his spirit and to overcome feelings of defeat or frustration. 07-5924-9 *Also on Tyndale Living Audio 15-7431-0*

SUCCESS! THE GLENN BLAND METHOD by Glenn Bland. The author shows how to set goals and make plans that really work. His ingredients of success include spiritual, financial, educational, and recreational balances. 07-6689-X

THROUGH GATES OF SPLENDOR by Elisabeth Elliot. This unforgettable story of five men who braved the Auca Indians has become one of the most famous missionary books of all time. 07-7151-6

TRANSFORMED TEMPERAMENTS by Tim LaHaye. An analysis of Abraham, Moses, Peter, and Paul, whose strengths and weaknesses were made effective when transformed by God. 07-7304-7

WHAT WIVES WISH THEIR HUSBANDS KNEW ABOUT WOMEN by Dr. James Dobson. A best-selling author brings us this vital book that speaks to the unique emotional needs and aspirations of today's woman. An immensely practical, interesting guide. 07-7896-0

WHAT'S IN A NAME? Linda Francis, John Hartzel, and Al Palmquist, Editors. This fascinating name dictionary features the literal meaning of hundreds of first names, character qualities implied by the names, and an applicable Scripture verse for each name. 07-7935-5

WHY YOU ACT THE WAY YOU DO by Tim LaHaye. Discover how your temperament affects your work, emotions, spiritual life, and relationships, and learn how to make improvements. 07-8212-7